PULLING TOGETHER

Crisis Prevention for Teens and Their Parents

Dr. Harold D. Jester

Mills & Sanderson, Publishers
Bedford, MA • 1992

Published by Mills & Sanderson, Publishers
41 North Road, Suite 201 • Bedford, MA 01730

Library of Congress Cataloging-in-Publication Data

Jester, Harold D., 1926-
Pulling together : crisis prevention for teens and their parents / by Harold D. Jester.
p. cm.
Includes bibliographical references and index.
Summary: A crisis-prevention manual intended to help teenagers get along with their parents and solve family difficulties without professional help.
ISBN 0-938179-30-6 : $9.95
1. Parent and teenager--United States. 2. Communication in the family--United States. [1. Parent and child. 2. Family life. 3. Conduct of life.] I. Title.
HQ799.15.J47 1992
649'.125--dc20 91-41371
CIP
AC

Printed and manufactured by Capital City Press.
Cover design by Lyrl Ahern.

Printed and Bound in the United States of America

To the memory of James F. Kneibler, my brother-in-law and lifelong friend, who was always affirming and supportive. We could not have been closer had we been brothers. For years he laughed at my stories and urged me to write—and for years I laughed at his suggestion. He would be pleased to know I finally settled down and followed his advice.

Acknowledgments

I wish to thank Thomas Gordon, Ph.D. and Effectiveness Training Inc. for permission to use information from their P.E.T. effectiveness training course in this book.

My wife, Marcia, has figured significantly in this production by her unfailing support, and by giving me valuable and constructive feedback during the many months of writing, revising and polishing. Thanks, Marcia!

I also want to acknowledge my indebtedness to the more than 2000 families in the greater Springfield, Massachusetts area with whom I have worked professionally since leaving the military in 1973. They have taught me much, and sustained my optimistic belief that people can change and do grow—even during difficult times.

Finally, I want to express my appreciation to publisher Georgia Mills, and managing editor Jan Anthony, of Mills & Sanderson, for what has been a most cordial relationship. Working with them has been like dealing with the folks next door. Their support, suggestions, enthusiasm and encouragement throughout the whole process has really been the most pleasant part of this endeavor. It served to put a warm human face on what must at times be a demanding and competitive business. I feel honored to have had them publish *Pulling Together*.

Foreword

At last we have a popular psychology book that brings parents and kids together in productive dialogue; this provides a springboard to conflict resolution where there are no losers, only winners! The style is serious, but the content is fast moving and peppered with humor. In fact, it is joyful, because it is not laborious. At the same time, it is on the cutting edge of the latest research in the field.

I like Dr. Jester's emphasis upon prevention and self-help because there has been too much reliance in the past upon what the professional does to fix things up. As we enter the twenty-first century, the thrust is in the direction of preventive education and group re-education, because the best results of counseling and therapy are achieved when clients can grasp and utilize the dynamic processes themselves. Real change never takes place in the office, but rather in the give and take of the inner sanctum of family life. Self-help is very useful then, because it enables some to bypass the expense of psychotherapy. For others, self-help complements therapy, and I see this book as serving the needs of both groups. I certainly plan to use it as an adjunct to my work with families.

Some funny things have happened on the way to the office over the past two decades. One of them is the growing appreciation on the part of clergypersons of all faith groups for the value and significance of the findings of psychology and psychiatry. The flip side of this is that clinicians have begun to pay more attention to the spiritual dimension of their clients and patients. Both professional groups seem to recognize that human growth and development is still a bewildering process. I like the way Dr. Jester has integrated the wisdom of his broad and diverse background as both clergyman and clinical psychologist.

In this book we see how adversarial debate as a style of communication is disruptive and needs to be replaced with self-revelation. With this, the need to intimidate and be right dissolves. I too find that at one time or another virtually every parent falls into the trap of asking, "Where did I go wrong?" and, "Why don't you?" I like the treatment of these issues. I also applaud Dr. Jester's emphasis upon the necessity for a family structure (house rules). Without these, the rudderless family vessel can easily founder, with the crew being tempted to abandon ship.

Pulling Together represents a significant contribution to the need for practical literature that will help to guide families on the journey to health, happiness and longevity.

Jacob Roseman

Jacob Roseman, M.D.
Medical Director, Western Region
Massachusetts Society for the Prevention of Cruelty to Children
Holyoke, Massachusetts

Director of Mental Health Services (Retired)
Wing Memorial Hospital
Palmer, Massachusetts

Preface

The structure presented in this volume is definitely workable. There is no doubt about that, for it evolved gradually and has been used successfully.

It is usually a crisis that brings families into my office; and I find that, as in a mattress fire, the underlying problem has often been smoldering for some time. A quick fix is rarely possible, and extended family counseling or therapy (I don't like either term) is both time consuming and expensive. In fact, it is increasingly costly at a time when health care costs are escalating and insurance benefits for outpatient mental health services are declining.

Community based family-life educational programs for young people and adults are certainly part of a possible answer, but they are still hard to sell and are of limited value after the mattress is blazing. It is this frustrating realization that caused me to start writing in this area several years ago. I felt that, at the very least, I could save my clients time and money by giving them material to read between sessions, which would explain and complement some of the things we did together in the office. This book expands upon a number of those individual handouts that I prepared. And who knows—if it is read before serious problems begin, it might even head them off. At least this is my hope.

My work suggests that one person cannot make a relationship work single-handedly. There must be a pulling together toward a shared objective—with meaningful payoffs for all along the way. That is what this book is all about.

Teenagers would surely benefit somewhat from reading Part One independently. Parents could read it and do likewise. But, for maximum benefit, parents and young people need to make the reading, discussion, and application of this material a joint venture.

Some parents will want to review it first, to determine just what it is that they're getting into. But where should they go from there?

The ideal approach, I think, is to launch this project preventively—*before* the barn door is open, before the mattress is blazing, before the storm clouds are directly overhead. Otherwise, expensive professional help may be needed to fix the situation. And let's face it—sometimes things happen in families that can't be fixed.

The way this is done will depend upon several variables: number, age, and sophistication of the children; time constraints; individual schedules; willingness of each participant to cooperate. There are also secondary concerns: frequency, place, and length of meetings, and the need to be free from interruptions (doorbells, pets, and telephone).

Under some circumstances, especially in the case of a single-parent, two families might make a joint project out of this. Another option is for two families (step, single-parent, or otherwise) to engage in a trade-off, with one or both adults from one family presiding over the meetings of the other family. But, in most cases, parents (or a single-parent) will be able to manage this without outside help.

A family might want to read and discuss its way through this book chapter by chapter at regular meetings, for experience has shown that it is unrealistic to expect every member of a group to read the material privately between sessions. And in order to facilitate such discussions, suggested questions are included in the appendix for possible use by the discussion leader, parent or otherwise.

We all seem to have a certain amount of built-in resistance to change, and this is understandable, for change is not always for the better. Then too, we tend to fear the loss of the power we have—or think we have—so patience is recommended here. If at this point a child (or children) refuses to cooperate, then the entire book should be read by the parent(s), and the structure implemented unilaterally. It may be necessary for some privileges to be suspended as an attention getter, or some rewards to be offered as an inducement to cooperation. But in most cases the cooperation will eventually come. If it doesn't, you might want to seek outside help to get things started; we'll discuss this more later.

If a family can work through this material together, and establish the suggested structure, certain benefits can be expected.

1. Young people and their parents will understand each other more, thus creating a foundation for healthier relationships.
2. Young people will understand how a family structure works to their advantage. They will see clearly that rules are necessary, and that every family member benefits from them.
3. Young people will come to accept a shared responsibility for the success of the family unit, which will alleviate the need for a parent to be in complete charge, together with all the headaches that go with that role.
4. Hassles, arguments, and conflicts will be dramatically reduced.
5. Self-reliance, self-respect, and family self-sufficiency will be enhanced. It all adds up to self-help at its best.

Part One is obviously inappropriate to put into the hands of young children. So, if there are no pre-teens or teenagers in the family yet, parents can still read it, implement the suggestions, and have it ready for the kids to read when they are old enough to understand it. That should be much easier for parents *and* kids than to write exclusively for adults, leaving it completely up to them to explain and interpret their program to the other members of the family.

Part Two, which is written just for parents, has its own introduction.

Table of Contents

PART ONE

Understanding and Getting Along with Parents

PART ONE

Understanding and Getting Along With Parents

About Part One ...

Many young people are tempted to give up on understanding their parents. At times Mom and Dad seem so transparent—on other occasions, absolutely beyond comprehension. Their moods appear to change with alarming speed and with no observable provocation whatever. No wonder children are genuinely mystified. Ask a parent what's wrong and you often get a gasp, followed by a confused stare, which roughly translates into, "You mean you don't know?" And if, in despair, you begin to mumble to yourself, you might even be accused of being a smart-mouth.

This book is dedicated to the proposition that this scenario does not have to be! Parents can be understood; they are not that complicated. And, may I add, you will be unable to really get along with them until you do understand them to some extent. So why not discover what makes parents tick? A little effort in this direction could pay rich dividends.

So what makes me think I understand your parents any better than you do? I'll tell you.

First of all, even though I am now 65 years old, I have a pretty good recollection of what my own childhood was like. This is so because I have been working on an autobiography for my children. By the time I was old enough to ask about the early memories of my parents, they were no longer around to share them: something they would gladly have done, had I cared enough to ask while they were still living. My autobiography will hopefully be available, although I shall probably not be, when my own children start to wonder about my past.

That process of writing has enabled me to recover many forgotten childhood experiences.

Secondly, I have been a father six times over. My youngest child, Michael, is now 12. My first child, Donald, died unexpectedly at age 2. Whatever I may have forgotten about parenting over the years is being relearned with Michael. I am sure I have learned from my experience, and I am equally sure that I am a better parent now—in some respects—than I was when Donald was born 43 years ago.

Thirdly, I have been a professional marriage and family counselor for a long time: 20 years as a chaplain in the United States Air Force, and 18 years as the director of a counseling center, following my return to civilian life. During this time my clients (men, women, young people and children) have been my best teachers, and I hope that I have been as good a student.

So, muddle through if you wish. Most of us did just that as young people, and we survived. But if you'd like to get a leg up on the situation, just read on.

Some statements and suggestions that I make here are not meant to be taken literally or followed slavishly. Rather, they are intended to be illustrative and to convey an impression or feeling. I do not suggest that all parents are impaired in the same way, or to the same degree, or even that all parents are impaired. I refer here to the average, garden-variety, American parent, if indeed there is such a person.

In reading what could sound like some worst-case scenarios in this book, two thoughts might be kept in mind. First, if you are equipped to deal with the worst, you'll probably sail through the rest. Second, I shall not deal in depth with the *really* worst-case scenarios (neglect and abuse), except to point out that they are in a class by themselves, requiring a very special and different response from children and the important people in their lives.

The chapters called *Where Did I Go Wrong?* and *Gladly Will I Toil and Suffer* deal with the subjects of guilt and suffering, respectively. I find that since I hold dual credentials as a clergyman and a clinical psychologist, I am able to make some judgments and observations about religion that a psychologist alone might be reluctant to make. For example, I would be less than honest if I suggested that it makes no difference what a person believes. It does matter! And there are plenty of unhappy people around who are trying to make their lives work, while they cling to irrational beliefs, religious and otherwise. But please remember: I am not criticizing anyone's church, denomination or faith group. I have lived long enough to know that there are some pretty wonderful people to be found within any religious body—as well as outside *all* religious bodies.

In addressing this to young people, I am taking a somewhat different approach to the development of healthy families than is usually chosen. Loads of books have been written that tell your parents how to succeed; but so often, something seems to get lost between the book and the children. This time, let's start with you, by laying out a humane and workable family structure that you can understand and support.

It's entirely possible that one of your parents may have read this before it reaches you. It is also possible that one or both of your parents may invite you to read and discuss this book as a *family project*. In such a case, try to cooperate with their efforts; you have nothing to lose and much to gain. But regardless of who reads it first, or how your family uses it, may this book help bring good family health to you all!

Some Basics

There are some underlying givens in parent-child relations which, if understood, can lessen the stress in your life and in the family. In this chapter some of these realities will be discussed, and suggestions will be offered for coping with them.

These issues can trap either you or your parents. And while there is no way you can keep your parents from screwing up, it still takes at least two people to fight. So being aware of these basics may help you to deflect a bad one that may be coming your way, or to avoid a land mine you're about to step on.

As you know from your experience with school teachers and principals, no one seems to care very much who started the fight once it is raging. To begin with then, let's consider...

The Need To Be Right

A Ph.D. philosophy professor and friend enjoys telling this story, the point of which is fairly clear.

He was attending an annual family reunion where a rather large number of people were gathered. A standard order of business at these affairs was to get caught up on recent happenings and to help process and embellish family myths.

Someone noticed that a particular couple was missing, and inquired about them. To this a more knowledgeable relative responded with, "Oh, haven't you heard? They are in the process of divorce!"

Seated on the sidelines was an elderly gentleman with a cane who gave little appearance of being completely tuned in. Instantly he came alive, moved to the edge of his chair, waved his cane in the air and exclaimed, "You remember, I told you 32 years ago when they married that it would never last!"

He had at last been vindicated by time, and it felt so good to be right.

My friend uses this incident as an example of what he believes to be a universal human need: the need to be right!

Mom and Dad probably have as great a need to be right as anyone. And since no parent could possibly be wrong all the time, you might want to be on the alert for behaviors that please you. Reinforce them quickly and appropriately with responses that will help parents feel that they can do something right at least once in awhile. Here are some usable reactions that anyone would be pleased to hear:

1. "Thanks (with a smile)."
2. "That really made me feel good."
3. "I really appreciated it when you (said or did so and so)."
4. "Know what, Mom? You were right when you said (whatever)."
5. "Dad, I thought about what you said; it does make sense."

One of the most frequent complaints I hear from parents is that they don't get enough recognition and appreciation, and consequently feel taken for granted. If you'd like to do something about this, move beyond simply responding positively to a behavior you like, and from time to time do something spontaneous and unexpected that will convey a sense of caring. The possibilities here are virtually limitless. And if you can learn to do this, you will make points for yourself like crazy. It will be like having money in the bank to draw on later.

I'm not sure just where the need to be right stacks up in any hierarchy of human needs, but I'm sure of this: no one likes to be told that he or she is wrong. You can make that judgment about yourself, but it is risky for another to do so.

No one, parent or child, is ever converted by a frontal assault, except superficially; and even then, we know that one convinced against his will is of the same opinion still. A person may yield under pressure to the greater power of another, but the humiliation will usually be remembered and resented until an opportunity is found to even up the score.

So if you feel that you're wrong, you might want to seize the moral high ground by admitting it. And if you are convinced that a parent is wrong, you might be well advised to avoid a direct confrontation. There is a better way, which we'll look at later. In the meantime, if you keep your cool, your parent may even calm down and acknowledge the error of his or her way quicker than if you point it out. If so, it could be a pleasant bonus.

Again, parents, like all people, have a need to be right and to avoid being wrong. So let's be honest and try to affirm them in whatever they do that is good or right. And let's try to resist the temptation to jump on them with both feet when we think they're wrong. To quote a well-known source, "A soft answer turneth away wrath."

Another basic concept in getting along with parents is to understand the dangers of attempted ...

Intimidation

I see this as a power play. It includes implied as well as overt threats. And, of course, it also includes giving an ultimatum. It inspires fear of unpleasant consequences if the other person fails to comply or conform.

Very few people are fully aware at the conscious level of just how much power they have. There is a valid place for power, and there are appropriate ways to use it—which we will discuss later. The point I should like to make here is simply that used thoughtlessly or recklessly, it can be very counter productive. Consider these risks if you try to intimidate another:

1. A threat or ultimatum is usually made impulsively or in anger. If, after you cool off, you want to back off from it, you could lose face. Better to think first!
2. The other person might escalate the conflict with a counter threat, thus complicating the situation and making it harder for you to disengage.
3. It could work and get you what you want, in which case you'll be tempted to use it again-and-again. At some point, however, in the home or outside, you'll run smack into a brick wall, with someone saying, "Go ahead, I'm tired of your extortion." And then,
4. Feeling trapped, you may have to go through with a threat even though you get hurt in the process. You could even conceivably wind up being dead right, as could easily have happened in the next case.

~ ~ ~

Alice bungled a half-hearted suicide attempt by firing her father's pistol into a sofa. Her parents were then so paralyzed by fear that they could not do enough for her. They were virtually unable to say no to anything. She was clearly in charge, and enjoyed every minute of it; and, with other children in the family, this soon created problems. For example, she was permitted to use the telephone for two hours each evening to talk with friends, which effectively cut her angry siblings out of any prime-time telephone use. The parents felt the other kids didn't understand, while they, in turn, were mad at their sister and accused the parents of being unfair.

I suggested to the daughter, in the presence of her parents, that it was surely only a matter of time until their fear would turn to anger. My concern was expressed this way, "When that happens, what are you going to do for an encore? With your back against the wall the only way to keep from losing face might be a serious suicide gesture." She got the point and gave up her strangle hold on the telephone for a shared and better arrangement.

~ ~ ~

Wait just a minute! you may say. Is it not equally important that parents not back their kids into a corner where they have no choice but to give in and lose face? Yes, indeed it is! But, unless your parents read this book too, that may not be an option and you may need to develop a defensive strategy for dealing with parental power plays. There will be more on this later. This brings us to the matter of ...

Direct Orders

Most people don't like being given direct orders by another person. But they will accept it under certain circumstances that they may have bought into: team sports, employment, and the military, for example.

This resistance to orders seems to be such a well known phenomenon that psychologists have learned to take advantage of it in psychotherapy, calling the strategy *paradoxical intention*. For example, a therapist might tell an obese new patient that he or she does not yet weigh enough to enter into treatment. It is prescribed that fifteen more pounds be gained before therapy begins, and a date is scheduled two weeks hence for another weigh-in. As if by magic, I am told, the patient returns two weeks later with a significant weight loss, based roughly upon the following thinking: "No one is going to tell me what I have to do; I'll lose weight if I want to. I'll show him!"

It's a scene right out of the Garden of Eden story, where God put a tree off limits and then, as Bill Cosby paraphrased it, Adam said, "Where, where?" He could hardly wait to get started!

As we see illustrated in both international and family events, no one who is fully human can be happy living in complete bondage to another. The yearning to breathe free is real!

In most families, the question of who's in charge has never been faced or negotiated. Parents just assume that they ought to be, while kids seem to assume that it's their job to fight it. And, not surprisingly, the tighter the attempted parental control, the greater the defiance from you kids.

In my home state the applicable laws hold parents responsible for establishing and enforcing rules that are both *reasonable and fair*. Obviously, the problem is to get all family members to agree as to what is reasonable and fair, but this is really a much easier process than one might think. There will be more on this later.

For now, let's focus on that knee-jerk reaction that makes kids want to engage in defiant reactions to parental orders, or instructions, or guidance, or whatever you want to call it.

It would certainly be nice if parents could learn to say please more often, and to ask courteously instead of barking orders. It would also be nice if parents could take more time to explain things rather than assuming so often that all kids are unreasonable. Yes it would be nice *if*; but the reality is that many kids have a sense of frustrated powerlessness because their parents don't treat them as they themselves would like to be treated. Sometimes adults even treat pets better.

I once began a talk to a parents group by reviewing an article from a current magazine on caring for one's pet. There were a dozen principles identified which, if followed, were supposed to lead to having a contented dog or cat. However, I told them that it was a list of guidelines for raising happy children, changing only a word or two here and there to make the list applicable to kids.

In response there was unanimous agreement that it would be great if we could follow those guidelines; and everyone wanted a copy. Then I told them the truth, but no one was mad at me for misleading them, for the message was obvious: if parents could treat kids at least as well as the family dog, they'd be off to a good start raising a family.

I guess I'm trying to point out that it is quite understandable for you to resent, and therefore to be tempted to blatantly defy, parental orders. It is the only obvious way to be sure that you are indeed a separate person with a mind of your own, rather than a Pinocchio with invisible strings attached.

Doubtless there are times when you would be totally justified in defying a parental order, but I suspect that in the vast majority of cases there are less risky ways to react. Sure, you can say, "I guess I showed them." But for the most part, you didn't really show them a thing. You just showed yourself, and maybe some peer witnesses—because you probably engaged in your defiance away from home. And if the behavior was dangerous, it could have been very self-defeating and even destructive. Following are some examples of what I mean—some serious, some humorous.

~ ~ ~

A father told his son, "One thing I could never forgive is if a son of mine ever got a girl pregnant." A few years later he did. Coincidence? Maybe.

~ ~ ~

A father sent his son to the barbershop for a haircut the teenager didn't want. The boy did a real butcher job cutting off his own hair, told his father he paid a friend to do it, and pocketed the five dollars. He then had to tolerate the ridicule of his friends.

~ ~ ~

A mother was preoccupied with a fear that her daughter would have sex before marriage. She moralized before the daughter's dates, and quizzed her after she returned home. Before long the girl became promiscuous, and soon started charging for her favors. Her explanation was, "I was getting accused of it—I figured I might as well be doing it and getting paid for it, too."

~ ~ ~

A son didn't want to attend public school on a particular day, so he took too much time getting ready and missed his bus. His mother then drove him to school, where he walked in the front door and right on out the back exit. When a school secretary called, the mother was sure her son was in school because she had personally delivered him.

~ ~ ~

In a local barbershop, I saw a young mother smile and say courteously to her 6-year-old, "Do me a favor: don't touch the blinds!" I thought that was strange because, although the child was close to the vertical blinds, he gave no appearance of being about to grab them. As soon as she spoke, he latched onto two panels with both hands—and with a vengeance!

~ ~ ~

So, what is the suggestion? Try to think before you act, and then act only in ways consistent with your best interests. That's a tall order, but the dividends are well worth the effort. You might think of it as acting, instead of reacting. When one reacts to the provocation of another, it is easy to do so defensively or in anger: both of which can be risky at best.

Summary

There is a sense in which this chapter attempts to point out that there are windows of opportunity presented that directly influence the quality of life in your family. You do not have to be a passive bystander. You can be an active and responsible contributor to your own well-being and to the health of your family system. You are not helpless; you are not a victim; you definitely have choices and options. And always, there are options that are constructive and creative. Always!

Ann Landers once told a large audience that she had heard of a new way to classify people. She said that in the first of three groups are the doers: the ones who are out there in the thick of things struggling to make things happen. Secondly, she said, there are those uncommitted, uninvolved observers who sit on the sidelines and watch things happen. Then, she concluded, there are those in that third group—the ones who ask, "What happened?"

You can and must, surely, want to live in that first group. In the chapters that follow, we will discuss more ways of bringing this about.

Where Did I Go Wrong?

> American parents are the most guilt-ridden parents in the whole world. They blame themselves for everything that goes wrong in the lives of their children. This differs markedly from the British system, which sees children as evil little monsters who must be tamed at great expense—and sometimes parents don't succeed.
>
> ***Margaret Mead***

We shall focus primarily upon parental feelings of guilt in this chapter, and I realize that at times guilt is mingled with fear, pity, and/or a sense of duty. In other words, *guilt* here is not used in a narrow or precise manner.

In considering the subject of guilt, I'd like to make a convenient distinction between two types. The first is that which an adult carries forward from the past, and I call it ...

Excess Baggage

It doesn't matter much what you've done or overlooked doing, a truly guilt-ridden parent will find some way to trace your real or imagined failure back to something he or she did wrong or failed to do right. There's not a lot you can do to change that, so you'd better accept what is and make the best of it. (This reminds me of a poster I once saw which said, "If life gives you lemons, learn to make lemonade.")

While it is difficult to say in every case just why a particular parent may have a heavy dose of guilt, some possibilities can not be easily dismissed. Early childhood training is certainly an obvious one. Take a good look at your grandparents, for example, if you would truly understand your parents. Children raised by overly strict, rigid, punitive parents with unusually high expectations, can hardly expect to reach maturity completely unscathed by their early formative experiences. Some even carry into adulthood a pervasive sense of inadequacy which spills over into their own parenting, and perpetuates the pattern. At some level a parent may partially glimpse this, and feel guilty.

On the other hand, a parent can carry excess baggage from the past in terms of desirable expectations that are just not completely workable in today's world. Take the case of those mothers who work outside the home—whether they are single or not, whether they want to or not. Very few families can survive comfortably on one income these days, but if your maternal grandmother did not work outside the home full time, your mother is in line for a real dose of guilt when she does so in order to provide for you. And if she is a single parent, her level of guilt is often unimaginably great. To deal with such situations requires a great deal of creative and cooperative thinking on the part of all family members, because there is no way a mother can return home exhausted after a full day at work, and expect to devote the rest of her waking hours to being supermom. And, single fathers have similar problems. There are simply not enough hours in the day for a mother (single or not) or a single father holding down a full-time job outside the home to be the type of interactive, involved parent they grew up with and stay sane, too!

Another possible explanation for parental guilt feelings can sometimes be found in the genetic component. The old proverb, "like parent, like child" holds considerable truth for these parents. How many times has a mother said in anger to her son, "You're just like your father!" She then goes on to ask herself why she ever married her husband in the first place, and so on and so on. It's all her fault that you screwed up, because she brought you into the world. Astute children have learned to latch on to this one with the now familiar conversation stopper, "I didn't ask to be born, did I?"

Still another variation on the genetic theme is that of a parent seeing his or her own unacceptable traits exhibited, and even magnified, in the behavior of the child. He or she then begins to pray, "My God, what have I done to this kid?" And then? You're right—more guilt!

I cannot count the number of times I have discussed this with a client who, usually weeping, has complained in words similar to these, "I always said I'd never grow up to be like my mother and treat my children the way I was treated; but every day I become more and more like her—and I am completely unable to stop it! I must be losing my mind; please help me."

Certainly, if we're to hypothesize on the origin of parental guilt, we can hardly afford to overlook the possible negative influence of some religious groups.

For instance, according to some of these groups, Jiminy Cricket was giving bad advice when he sang in the Disney film version of Pinocchio, "... And always let your conscience be your guide." Their viewpoint says, in effect, that you cannot trust your conscience, because it is flawed, but you can trust their organization's judgment, because it is not. They claim to have an inside track with God, and thus to speak only the truth. Conformity is the order of the day!

Strangely, over the years these same religious groups have moved from one infallible position to another, while the faithful are not supposed to entertain doubts or break ranks. To deviate or to think for one's self is very risky, and causes considerable guilt.

If Margaret Mead is correct in labeling American parents as the most guilt-ridden in the world, the American religious scene has undoubtedly had at least something to do with it.

So how do you go about making lemonade when you hear a vague, "Where did I go wrong?" First of all, you might want to remember that your parent is probably looking for reassurance or sympathy. And this is what you will be tempted to give. After all, who enjoys seeing an adult cry? Especially one's mother or father?

But is this an appropriate response, especially when you may be looking at only the tip of the guilt iceberg? A little bit of sympathy never hurt anyone, but too much hand holding may cause you to feel that the roles are reversed, with you functioning more as the parent. If you fall into this trap, you will surely wind up blaming and resenting your parent for it.

Beyond the immediate need of the moment, the guilt-ridden person wants more than sympathy. When a parent believes that he or she has failed you, there is a need felt to make up for it in some way: to appease you, placate you, pacify you. In other words, to atone for the sin. And no sacrifice is too great! Parents will gladly burn themselves out and spend themselves broke for their children, if it helps to neutralize the guilt.

Is it any wonder then that some young people suppress the impulse to show mercy? They know the problem is bigger than the moment, and suspect that there is little they can do about it. So, playing the role of the accommodating opportunist, they choose to go with the flow and exploit parental guilt for personal gain. It is easy to do, and I have witnessed it often.

Opportunists don't ask if it's right. They don't consider the long-term consequences. They ask only if it will get them what they want at the moment.

I'm sure you're familiar with the standard tricks. They have been around for so long that it's surprising they still work, but I continue to see them almost every day:

1. Sulking, or withdrawal into silence. It drives most parents absolutely bonkers, especially if you miss a meal.

2. The I-don't-understand routine, where the parent keeps on trying to make you understand, and you keep on pretending to be dense. Eventually the parent gets exasperated and exhausted, and frequently gives in to your demand.
3. Tears, accompanied by, "Nobody understands me."
4. Any plea that begins with the words, "If you love me ..."
5. A complaint introduced by, "You're the only parent I know who expects a kid to ..."
6. Threats like, "I don't think I can take one more day of this."

Now, I have no problem understanding how kids get into the habit of using these tricks, but I must share with you three monstrous problems with this approach:

1. No young person can really respect a parent who tolerates such behavior, because it is seen as weakness, and kids expect good parents to exhibit strength.
2. No young person can respect himself or herself for engaging in such calculated and manipulative behavior. It feels like taking coins out of a blind beggar's cup.
3. Once started, it's a tough habit to break.

But before we place all the blame on children for not making the best choices, and thus getting into bad habits, we should remember that even nice kids can be driven to become opportunists by parents who are crowding them too much and leaning on them too hard, and who may need to be cut down to size, as only you kids can do! But I guess I would like you to know that there are other options that carry less risk. Let's look at them now.

Any developmental and adjustment problems your parents have were with them long before you came along. Your birth only gave them more to cope with, and maybe they were not fully prepared for the task, especially if you are the only or oldest child in the family. Hopefully they are going to learn from what goes on between you and them, but that does not make you responsible for solving all the problems they may have with the relationship, even though at times it may look to you as if you are.

It often works like this: a parent is displeased with a behavior of yours and somehow manages to blame himself. You feel sorry for him and then begin to feel guilty, too, for *making him* unhappy. Then you feel responsible for fixing it, so he'll be happy again, even though you may see nothing wrong with your original behavior.

As I have already tried to point out, you always have more than one option in any given situation—so do your parents! But too often, for a number of reasons, no one takes the time to explore them. So, you are not responsible for solving their problems. You are fully responsible for *your* own behavior, but not for how your *parent* reacts to it or feels about it. That is his or her choice. This does not mean that it's okay to be indifferent to parental needs and feelings; just that you didn't necessarily cause them, and you sure can't solve them all by yourself—no matter what you do. Maybe you can help your folks, but the full burden of responsibility for a solution must not rest upon your shoulders.

This can be seen in divorce cases where kids often blame themselves for causing the separation, followed by a sense of responsibility for getting the parents back together again.

What Margaret Mead says about American parents may also be true for American kids. So let your parents own their problems, while you own yours; and it is very important to keep this distinction in mind. Don't get sucked into parental guilt by taking advantage of it, or by feeling that you caused it, or that you're responsible for fixing it. So much for what not to do; now for what you can do.

I recently reconnected with a childhood friend I had not seen for 40 years, and we had a great time reminiscing. As a young man he was relaxed, friendly, and always able to laugh; so much so that some adults told him he should be less frivolous and more serious if he ever wanted to amount to anything. Today he is a highly successful professional person with the same beautiful sense of humor, and as he looked back upon the constellation of people who influenced both of us in very profound ways, he observed, "But there's one thing I hold against them: they all wanted me to grow up too fast."

It's not just okay to have a keen sense of humor; it is, in my opinion, absolutely essential! Kipling said, "If you can keep your head when all about you are losing theirs, and blaming it on you ... you'll be a Man, my son!"

If you can keep your cool and maintain your sense of humor with your parents, and resist the temptation to take them too seriously, you'll be able to react creatively when one of them moans something like, "Where have I failed?" Remember—with a smile; no sarcasm. Examples? Here are a few that have come to my attention out of real life:

1. "You mean you don't know?"
2. "Do you really want to know?"
3. "I've been trying to figure that one out too."
4. "At last you are beginning to make some sense."
5. "Considering who your mother is, you're probably doing the best you can."
6. "Have you considered getting professional help?"

A word of caution is in order on that last one. Like manipulative kids, some clergy need guilt-ridden parishioners in order to stay in business; so they will only offer short-term relief through prayer and ritual, much like you take aspirin for a headache. Long-range help with deep-seated or inappropriate guilt will probably best be found with a licensed mental health worker or a clergyperson who has had extensive clinical training.

In addition to a good sense of humor there is more that you can do. Take care of yourself. Learn to like yourself, for you are absolutely unique; value that uniqueness. Connect with others who like you and who affirm your uniqueness. And if your parents fit into this category, you will be of all people most blessed, because the messages of those who get to us first in life are the most indelible, persistent and influential. Richard Nixon learned the hard way that you can record a new message on a previously used tape, but that process never completely erases the earlier messages. With proper equipment they can all still be read. It is prudent therefore to have in your own memory banks the best possible memories about yourself, for if they are bad they may screw up your life for years to come—and maybe for life! The star of *Pretty Woman* said, "The bad stuff is easier to remember." In her case that was so because her earliest memories from life with mother were pretty negative. Don't depend too much on others or permit others to depend too much on you. Learn to handle being alone without being lonely. Don't be afraid to struggle, and avoid like the plague the person who responds to your inevitable periods of uncertainty with the confident call, "I can see the way; follow me."

We've been looking at *excess baggage*: the feeling of guilt or inadequacy a parent carries forward from the past. Now let's consider what might be called ...

Situational Guilt

This arises from that category of kid-behavior that seems to provoke or trigger some kind of excessive or inappropriate parental response which then leaves the parent feeling guilty for what he or she has done. Of course it may be argued that if the parent didn't have some excess baggage to begin with, he or she wouldn't be so vulnerable to situational guilt. I agree with this, and acknowledge that I am treating the subject this way only in order to make it easier to deal with.

~ ~ ~

> At the breakfast table a young mother raises her voice to her child, who responds by clumsily knocking over a glass of milk, and shouting back, "Look what you made me do!" The child is alert to the possibilities of the moment, determined not to let his mother get the best of him. And you know what? It works; and the mother immediately assumes it was an accident she caused by rattling him. She then feels guilty and apologizes profusely as she cleans up his mess. At a very tender age this precocious little kid has learned how to push his mother's guilt button to get exactly what he wants. He is in charge now and the next move is up to him. The rules of this game are two. The first is, whoever gets mad first loses, as long as the winner does not respond in kind. The second is that having caught his mother in an ugly act, the child is entitled to one wish, to even up the score. If he doesn't settle for small potatoes he can get a lot of mileage out of it.

~ ~ ~

Left unchecked, this look-what-you-made-me-do posture can be carried through to the teen years and beyond, with the drunk, the junkie, the criminal, the misfit, and the marginal performer saying to his parents, spouse, employer, or society in general, "Look what you made me do!" It is a very debilitating and self-defeating attitude. But it is easy to see how innocently it gets started.

Let's look at the example closely. Mother yells at her son, who is unable or unwilling to say, "Gee, Mom, I don't like it when you yell at me." Since he can't or won't talk about his feelings, he acts them out by spilling the milk and creating work for her.

This is typical of what is called *passive aggressive* behavior. It is a roundabout, oblique, indirect way of getting back at another person. But to make sure she doesn't misunderstand, he adds, "Look what you made me do!" The clear message then is, Mom—lay off!

Have you ever engaged in passive aggressive behavior? Of course you have. We all have, and we all probably still do from time to time. Following are some pretty typical examples of what I mean:

1. Never completely emptying something in the refrigerator, but leaving a little bit so that someone else has to clean up the container;
2. Going off and leaving your clothes in the drier;
3. Draining all the hot water from the tank during a shower;
4. Taking a few sections of the newspaper off somewhere and forgetting to return them;
5. Going to sleep with your bedroom radio playing just loud enough so that Mom or Dad has to turn it off;
6. Insisting on using the telephone in your parents' bedroom, claiming that you *must* have privacy;
7. Borrowing the car, but claiming you forgot to replace the gasoline;
8. Even if you have homework, insisting that there's plenty of time to complete it in study hall;
9. Leaving your dirty clothes in a pile on the floor, with a wet towel or two in the heap, just for laughs;
10. Eating in your room and failing to return the dishes to the kitchen;
11. Asking to be paid in advance for work you are then too busy to do.

This list is for starters. With only a little effort you'll be able to recall dozens of things you have done to push a parental ugly button.

Now here's my concern, and I'll approach it from two directions. The first is that in talking to young people I've seen cases, again and again, where one has engaged chronically in passive aggressive behavior that does not seem to be in response to a specific provocation like the breakfast routine I described. It seems rather to be more generalized, almost like a pattern, or an established way of relating to parents. It looks suspiciously like defiance for defiance sake, like I described in the previous chapter.

The other direction comes from parents who say something like: "I feel so guilty for the way I just seem to pick, pick, pick on my child."

Could it be that parent(s) and child have unwittingly become locked together in some kind of a mutually destructive way of relating to each other, with no one knowing how to escape from it? In some cases this must be so.

Could it be a way to avoid the risks and challenges of intimacy by keeping each other at arm's length? This is also probably so in some cases.

I know of one mother who said that the first responsibility of a parent was to break the will of the child. In such a case, could a child's chronic passive aggressive behavior be a survival mechanism? Of course—sometimes.

These possibilities do not cover all the situations I have seen. And I wonder about this as an explanation: could it be that some kids use passive aggressive behaviors simply to keep a vulnerable parent off balance? If so, it works, because it invites nagging, which then results in guilt for the nagging parent, which can then be exploited by the opportunistic child for personal advantage. And by the way, this can all go on without ever reaching the conscious level of the mind. But sometimes it can be completely conscious and calculated, as in the following case, where a 16-year-old boy confesses to having this down to an exact science. He said, ...

> I found that silence and a pained expression can often be more powerful than words. If I follow this with a withdrawal to my room, it will give the process a chance to work without further aggravation from me. When my parent can stand the isolation no longer, there will be a knock at the door. This is my first opportunity. There will be at least one more. I am careful not to blow either one. The first one may be an occasion for a gift: my favorite snack, or a promise of some kind. I smile a little, but don't recover completely from my pain. The second opportunity will come the next time I ask for something: use of the car, a late late night out, whatever. I don't squander my request on small change, but I'm not unreasonable either. If my request is not outlandish, it will probably be granted, and that will balance things out for this time in the mind of my parent.

A fellow like this will rarely become a valued friend, but he could grow up to become a successful lawyer.

And what's the point? We had better all learn to *talk* out our problems with others rather than to *act* them out. Acting them out in passive aggressive ways is dangerous for a number of reasons. Here are just a few, in conclusion:

1. The message is never completely clear; it is always blurred to some extent. As such, what the parent hears may be inaccurate.
2. Therefore, the problem does not get resolved; it only gets worse for both parties.
3. Destructive and self-defeating habits are developed, which will lead to greater problems in the future.

Summary

In this chapter we have focused upon guilt in an attempt to understand parents, and thereby increase the chances for relating to them in healthier, more successful ways. We considered the excess baggage parents often carry with them from childhood, and examined how this makes them highly vulnerable to destructive encounters with their children. It was suggested that young people, while fully responsible for their own behavior, cannot and should not be blamed or held responsible for the choices, actions and feelings of their parents.

I suggested that a good sense of humor is indispensable to a quality relationship with one's parents, and that the easiest way to fail is to try to live up to another person's plan for one's life.

The temptation to manipulate parental guilt for one's own advantage was recognized, as well as the potentially catastrophic consequences that await the one who consistently yields to this temptation.

Next, we'll consider another subject that is closely connected to guilt. In fact, it is difficult to make clear-cut subject divisions in this book, because there is a sense in which everything is connected to everything else. To some extent, then, these chapters will overlap, and will not be mutually exclusive.

Gladly Will I Toil and Suffer

> With one look a child can get the candy bar you were saving for yourself or get you to take the bent fork or the egg with the broken yolk ...
> Scarcely a day goes by that we don't read a story about the sacrifices parents make on behalf of their children ... We buy cookies from children when we're on a diet, chaperone weekends that add years to our lives, plan our meals around their sports schedules, and sell our blood for the newest Nintendo game.
>
> *Erma Bombeck*

Why? Out of love and devotion? Of course! Because childhood should be a happy time? Perhaps. As some kind of perverse investment in the future, when it will be paid back with interest in the parents' old age? Sometimes.

So what's wrong with it? Nothing, so long as it is kept in balance, with the parents getting their fair share now and then.

Nothing is wrong with it unless putting kids first becomes so much a pattern that they think they deserve it and have it coming to them as a right, as in the following story.

~ ~ ~

> Two families were spending a week with us at our island retreat: a small piece of paradise in northern Vermont. There were ten of us all together, including one teenager in each of the three families, plus my then-7-year-old son.

When the breakfast call was sounded for our first meal together, the hungry young men—with my 7-year-old close behind—rushed in from outside and laid claim to four of the six chairs around the only table.

With just two places left, the six adults were too polite to seat themselves, and just stood around waiting. Meanwhile the boys wolfed down whatever food they could get their hands on, never once offering anything to any adult. There were moans and groans from them when my wife finally cut them off and chased them out of the cabin. Then the rest of us ate. The other five adults just seemed to accept this as normal kid behavior and said nothing about what we had just witnessed; but I silently determined that I would even things up, come dinner time.

The evening meal included barbecued chicken, with plenty of food for all. It was to be eaten outside on the deck where there was an adequate number of lawn chairs and snack tables. When I announced that the chicken was ready, the three older boys expectantly surrounded the grill with their plates at arm's length, waiting to be served.

I quietly said, "Fellows, this evening your parents get served first!"

I was not prepared for what happened next—one of the boys jumped straight up in the air, came down and stormed over to his father, shouting, "That's not fair; there won't be anything left for us!" His father did not respond. In fact, nothing was said, as the adults, each with a smile, lined up to be served.

That young man's attitude shocked even his parents. And after dinner father and son took a long walk together, for some long-overdue conversation.

~ ~ ~

He was no worse than the other two teenagers—just more vocal. Not one of the teenagers saw anything wrong with their behavior at breakfast and dinner. So, if this is typical behavior, why do we parents let our kids get away with it?

For a part of the answer I think we need to go back to the previous chapter where I said, "No sacrifice is too great! Parents will gladly burn themselves out and spend themselves broke for their children because it helps to neutralize the guilt." There is even a popular hymn that says, "Gladly will I toil and suffer, only let me walk with thee."

There is another one I learned as a young person in summer camp that spelled JOY as, "Jesus and Others and You," and suggested that you, "put yourself last and spell JOY."

It is easy to be misled by such notions, and it does seem to be clear that the masses frequently fail to examine critically what is being offered to them for consumption. When this happens, some unfortunate things can result.

For example, if a woman endures chronic abuse from an alcoholic husband, while she struggles single-handedly to keep the family together for the sake of the children, many people will call her a saint.

If, in a parents' discussion group, a mother or father is excited over how well things are going at home, he or she quickly learns not to acknowledge that, for it is too threatening to the others, who tend to compete with one another for the *Horror Story of the Week Award.*

~ ~ ~

> A young man who was just concluding his junior year in college went to the family physician for a premarital blood test. The good doctor shook his head at the end of the visit and said, "You sure proved me wrong! I always said you'd never amount to anything."
>
> All the doctor knew about the boy had been gleaned from the comments of his parents, primarily his mother. She was so proud as she complained to him of the pain she suffered at the hands of her unappreciative boy.

> Her son was the cross she carried nobly, glad for a chance to toil and suffer in a righteous cause, and sure that there would be stars in her crown in heaven.
>
> But you know what? That young man succeeded in spite of the dire predictions of his mother and the physician. And, of course, his mother claimed credit for every bit of his success.

~ ~ ~

One of the interesting characteristics of this kind of religious mentality is that it has a nice, neat, pat answer for everything. And, if we are to believe the statistics and studies, rather than dying out, it is spreading.

While American rabbis encourage their congregations to realize that they live in a Christian nation, Christian clergy bemoan what they see to be an increasing secularization of the country, for which they deny responsibility.

Meanwhile, some sociologists see the development of a true secular religion that borders on becoming almost a state church. One of the characteristics of this alleged secular religion is that by osmosis it has picked up some of the best and worst of institutionalized religion. One result of this is that an excessive guilt and a willingness to toil and suffer one's way into goodness can be found in folks both inside and outside of religious institutions. In fact, several studies have suggested that with respect to ethics and moral standards, there is no measurable difference between those who are identified with a religious community of some kind, and those who are not.

This is probably what led Margaret Mead to remark that, "American parents are the most guilt-ridden parents in the whole world," as I noted earlier.

This brings us pretty much full circle on the subject of understanding parental guilt and suffering, except for the question of what kids can do, if anything, about dealing with it in parents and others.

Some of the suggestions made in the last chapter are applicable here, too: don't get sucked into it; maintain your sense of humor; live responsibly; and resist the temptation to exploit it. I know it is very tempting to join forces with the young man who said to me, "If my dad is determined to suffer, why not let him do it for a worthy cause—me! It makes him feel so much better afterward." But difficult as it may be, the prudent teenager will try to maintain a respectful detachment from parental guilt and suffering.

Since I have taken a few swipes at some forms of institutionalized religion, I want to balance it off with this: A synagogue or church can be, ought to be, and in some cases is, the strongest force for mental health in the community. I grew up in one that was, and if you are fortunate enough to be a part of such a religious community, I am indeed happy for you.

But suppose you feel really uncomfortable in your parents' religious group, what can you do?

Here are some possibilities:

1. I know of one girl who said, "I take my religion much too seriously to go to church." Others have simply refused to go, and insisted on staying home, or going somewhere else with a friend. These actions generally meet with a variety of parental responses, rarely positive.

2. You might try being honest with your parents about it. I know a young person whose parents responded to this by admitting that they shared similar feelings. Then together they began looking for a new church home.

3. One enterprising youth wanted to stop going to church altogether, but was sure his parents would disapprove. So he found a job where he could work on Sunday mornings. That was a real stroke

of genius, in my opinion, because it's rare for even the most devout parent to stand in the way of a youngster's earning money. That would be positively un-American.

4. Whatever you do, you might want to keep on looking instead of settling for something second rate. Remember, the question of which church is *the right one* is never valid. Which church, if any, is the right one for *you* is more like it.
5. If you choose to profess yourself an atheist, humanist, agnostic, or whatever, that's your right, too. Just be careful about going too far out on a limb or burning too many bridges behind you. You might find it hard to back off from your pronouncements later on if you should change your mind. And finally ...
6. Try to remember that boundaries between denominations, and even major faith groups, are not as rigid or clear cut as they once were—at least in this country. They are more like permeable membranes. Neither do the names of particular religious bodies, or their creeds, necessarily say very much about the thinking and posture of the leaders and members of a local branch of that larger group.

Summary

The last two chapters have dealt with the interlocking issues of guilt and suffering, and we have considered how this can complicate the parent-child relationship.

Being alert to these dangers will enable you to practice the kind of preventive maintenance that can raise the overall level of your happiness by several notches. But, of course, there is much more to come.

In the last chapter, I referred to some ploys used by opportunists in their attempts to manipulate others. One of them began with the words that have become the title for our next chapter ...

If You Love Me You Will

These words have served as a preface for a wide variety of heavy-handed efforts to get what we want from one another. Here are just a few examples of how my clients have completed the conditional statement, "If you love me you will ..."

... let me do that.

... not disappoint me.

... remember my birthday.

... do what I ask.

... let me choose my own clothes.

... remember what I tell you.

... stop that nasty habit.

... not go out with that boy.

Ever heard anything like that before? Ever said something like that? Of course—on both counts, I am sure. Notice, please, just how easy it is for either a parent or a child to lean hard on another person in the name of love. It is not only easy to say such things, it is also dreadfully easy to cave in if you're on the receiving end of that kind of pressure. And afterward you feel like you've been had.

But either way, everybody loses, and here's why:

1. The one who says things like this to you is undermining your moral authority, and is relocating it in the hands of another, who is presumably wiser, more knowledgeable, or more experienced. This is demeaning.

2. If you allow another person to make these judgments for you, will you ever get the authority back? And if so, when? How difficult will it be to reclaim it?
3. If you are the one who makes these statements, do you want, and will you be able to handle, the dependency it creates? For as long as a person has to check with another to see what should be done, he or she will never become self-reliant.
4. You can tell another person what you would like him to do, but not what he *ought* to do, unless it's a threat. And we know what threats do to people, don't we? It often results in their becoming defiant.
5. Another person can tell you what is illegal, but not what you *ought* to do.
6. Another person can warn you of impending danger, but not tell you what you *ought* to do about it.

The message in all of these examples seems to be, if you love me, trust me to tell you what you ought to do, for I know what is best for you. In addition to the six things I identified as being wrong with that, there is an additional risk in that at times it can be downright dangerous, if not life threatening, as in the following case. This story is not strictly an if-you-love-me tale; rather it illustrates the risk involved in blindly yielding to the bidding and authority of another.

~ ~ ~

My wife's Uncle Edwin was a delightful gentleman and gifted artist until he lost his eyesight; then he turned to writing. A number of his essays were published under the title, "I Don't Remember Getting Born." One of the stories told of an experience in Boston after he stepped from a bus onto the crowded sidewalk at a busy intersection. He stood there trying to sense whether it was safe to cross, when a powerful hand grasped his arm, and a confident voice shouted, "Now!" And together they charged across the street. Tires screeched, horns honked, and a driver shouted obscenities--but they made it safely to the other side. Only then did Uncle Edwin discover that his Good Samaritan was also blind.

~ ~ ~

This raises a good point. In a world of blind people, a one-eyed man may indeed be king, but when you are blind and someone says, "I can see; follow me," how can you be sure that person can really see? Or that he or she has better vision than yours? Or that your would-be benefactor doesn't have an even greater handicap that makes following him or her dangerous? Like a lack of good judgment; or worse yet, a lack of integrity?

I saw an office sign once that read, *Whoever can remain calm in the midst of all this confusion simply doesn't understand the situation.* And in another setting, a sign read, *When in danger, fear or doubt, run in circles, scream and shout.* But the prize will still go to you—if, as Kipling suggested, "... you can keep your head when all about you are losing theirs and blaming it on you." And we may add, telling you what you *ought* to do about it.

Speaking of signs, I like the one I saw above the desk of a welfare department social worker who was doing intake work. It immediately had a calming effect upon the new applicant she was interviewing in my presence. It read, *Your failure to plan ahead does not necessarily constitute an emergency for me.*

I think she had caught the spirit of the frazzled man, approaching burnout while doing good, who was quoted in a recent issue of "Yokefellows" newsletter as saying, "I have had a stroke of sanity. I now see that I am not responsible for any other person, or his or her welfare. I am responsible only to express *agape*-love to that individual, and *on my own terms,* for only I know how much time, energy, and money I have available to expend."

His point is well taken. Each of us has finite resources: time, energy, materiel. If we allow others to dictate the terms for our management of these limited assets, we will soon spin out of control and crash. And, as one of my former base commanders used to say, "Remember, it's not the fall that hurts; it's the sudden stop!"

Is it a new concept to be told that it's okay, and even a duty to love yourself? It's really as old as the oldest continuously functioning religion in the world, Judaism. Jesus, himself a good Jew, summarized it this way in response to a question as to which commandment was the most important:

> The first is, "Hear, O Israel: The Lord our God, the Lord is One; and you shall love the Lord your God with all your heart and with all your soul and with all your mind and with all your strength."
> The second is this, "You shall love your neighbor as yourself." There is no other commandment greater than these.

I wish I had heard more of this as a kid, and less of, "Put yourself last and spell JOY."

When we speak of self-love, we're not referring to the seeking of personal gain at the expense of another; that is admittedly, among other things, downright selfish. Neither are we suggesting that life is to be lived with reckless abandon. "It's my life, isn't it?" may in one sense be true, but there's little to be gained by being dead right about it. What is meant is more in keeping with the concept of enlightened self-interest, or perhaps more accurately, self-respect.

There are strange things done in the name of love. Marauding armies have fought, killed, raped, pillaged, maimed, looted, and burned—all in the name of love!

An enraged husband recently beat his wife senseless and declared, "I love that woman more than anything else in the whole world; and I only slap her around a little when it's necessary—to keep her in line."

Parents physically abuse their children and explain to them, "This really hurts me more than it does you, but I'm doing it for your own good because I love you."

Two otherwise sensible people have been known to run off and get married on the basis of little more than a pleasant weekend together—because they are in love!

A crime is committed by a man who then comes home and says, "I did this because I love you, baby."

I have come reluctantly to the conclusion that the power of the human mind to repress, forget, suppress, distort, rationalize, justify, fabricate, and confabulate is almost limitless. Yet with all its limitations, it is the only mind you will ever have. And if you are to be truly responsible for your behavior, you have no choice but to try to make as many of your own decisions as possible. Get input from others; learn as much as you can from the experience of others; read what you can get your hands on; discuss it with friends; defer judgment for a time, if appropriate. But when it comes time for the decision, let it be yours!

You may accept the mandate to love everyone, friend, foe and self alike, but you'll be on thin ice if you ever allow someone else to define the terms on which you express that love. That is your privilege, and, indeed, your responsibility, and it is *yours alone.* It is important to remember that, lest we unwittingly violate another or allow another to violate us in the name of love.

If you make a decision that you later conclude was a bad one, remember that it doesn't make you a bad person. In fact, the only way to avoid bad decisions is to avoid *all* decisions. The healthy thing to do with mistakes is to accept responsibility for them, learn from them, and correct or make restitution for them where possible.

Flo said to Andy Capp, "You know what? You're a flippin' failure!"

Andy jumped to his feet and shouted back, "How can I be, woman? I've never tried."

I don't know of any ethical code that asks any more of you than that you do the best you can with what you have at any given moment.

Perhaps you may be determined not to pull the if-you-love-me bit with your parents; but how do you deal with it if one of them doesn't know any better than to use it on you? I can only offer some possible responses, knowing that you will think of others. You might say, for example:

1. "I love you, but I'm not sure what that has to do with this."
2. "I love you, but if I do as you ask, I'll feel violated."
3. "It seems pretty important to you that I do as you say."
4. "If I do as you ask, I'm not sure what that will do to me."
5. "If I do as you ask, I'll feel that you have won and I have lost."
6. "I don't know how to respond to you. I need time. Can we talk more about it later?"

This last one is useful for giving you time to think, without the pressure of the moment. But as useful as any of these responses might be, none of them will do much more than protect you temporarily. To do the best job, you'll need to have well developed communication skills in the areas of listening, confrontation, and conflict resolution. Again, more on this later.

It's beyond the scope of this book to adequately cover the full nature and meaning of love, but let's touch on on some closely allied issues that can be troublesome if misunderstood.

Why Did You?

Sometimes, in a tone that suggests displeasure, a parent or a child asks the other why he or she did a certain thing. Clearly implied, although not always spoken, is something more like, "If you love me, (or, if you trust me, or, if you respect my parental authority) then why did you do what you did?" There appears here to be a clear expectation on the part of one disappointed person that the other individual should not have behaved in a certain way.

When this happens in my office I often ask where that expectation comes from. And what we usually discover is that it is rooted in previous experience: family of origin, reading, movies or TV, behavior of friends, or something one picked up during the course of his religious or secular education.

Until we see evidence to the contrary, most of us just assume that all wives, husbands, parents, or kids should be expected to behave in certain prescribed ways. And when, for the first time, another person fails to treat us in accordance with our stereotypes, we're inclined to take it personally and ask why.

If you are asked to explain yourself to another, when you did not violate an agreement with him or her, you might try to resist the temptation to become defensive. Instead, you might say something like, "I don't think we ever discussed or negotiated that; I didn't deliberately try to upset you—let's talk about it." Here again, a soft answer will soothe hurt feelings—hopefully.

And while we're on the subject of expectations, let's pursue it further and ask what, if anything, we have a right to expect from another person.

Somewhere around 1982, I read a brief article on the front cover of a church newsletter which was written by a friend. In it the author convincingly suggested that we should not have *any* expectations of others; but rather, he said, we should love and accept people as they are! I felt uneasy about that, and brought it up in a weekly therapy group which I was leading.

Without exception, everyone present rejected the essay. And that launched us on a project that we worked on for several weeks. It didn't consume a great deal of our time, but we developed and polished a document on the subject until there was a consensus on the content. And what follows is an expression of the basic expectations those men and women had for any relationship that they cared about. I share it and suggest that you review it carefully. You might want to discuss it with your family and trusted friends, and modify it where necessary, in order to come up with a list of your expectations of others with whom you are involved in some caring way.

Expectations ...

1. We will accord each other common every-day courtesies, respect, civility, and good manners.
2. We will constantly work to maintain open and clear channels of communication.
3. Together we will cultivate and nurture that common area of activities, concerns, and interests which binds us together.
4. We will hold to a mutual loyalty and tolerance when it comes to those foibles which become obvious because of our proximity.
5. We will honor mutual agreements and not change our commitments without negotiation or notification. We should be reliable, dependable, and predictable when it comes to our commitments and agreements.
6. We will try not to make assumptions of any kind. If it has not been discussed or negotiated, it will not be taken for granted.

7. Each of us will maintain a healthy measure of detachment, autonomy, and enlightened self-interest, never losing our individual identities. We will have our separate goals, take pride in ourselves and in our own achievements, and be prepared to function independently, so that we do not become overly dependent upon each other for the satisfaction of our individual needs.
8. Each of us is free to ask anything of the other, but only for so long as we are willing to accept a *no* for an answer. Otherwise the request becomes a demand.
9. We will honor a mutual veto rule. This means that we do together only what we are both willing to do together, and only for so long as we are both willing to do it.
10. We will not lie to or otherwise deliberately deceive the other. This undermines trust, which is essential to our relationship. This does not mean that we are open to interrogation by the other, or that we are not entitled to privacy—including private thoughts—just that whatever we choose to express will always be the truth.

Now for a few specific comments on these. The following numbers refer back to the same numbers on the previous list:

3. If we fail to do this in the family we wind up with only a collection of people.

5. It is very easy to agree to anything, just to end a discussion, like signing a legal document without reading the fine print. But let's be careful about what we agree to, lest we appear later to be undependable.

7. Every relationship you have will eventually end. Sooner or later one of you will die, relocate or lose interest.

8. My third son taught me this one when he was only 12 years of age. I asked him to take out the trash, and he responded with, "Sure Dad; just as soon as this TV program is over." I replied, "No; I mean right now. You forgot it completely last week." He did as I asked, saying simply, "In that case, why did you ask me? Why didn't you just tell me?" I never forgot that.

10. This one requires more space, keep it in mind, and I will deal with it in the next chapter.

Let's suppose now that you like this list of expectations, or a similar one of your own that you may have developed. Where do you go with it from here?

In most families there are unwritten and, frequently, unspoken rules that are nevertheless known by all members, and that serve to guide individual behavior. Strictly speaking, these expectations are not a list of family or house rules, but simply a set of expectations that I believe you have a right to hold in any caring relationship. However, even if you wanted to, you probably would not get away with handing it to your parents or to a friend, with the announcement that this is what you expect from them.

You might, however, find others receptive if you share your list as something you can personally commit yourself to follow. Offer to discuss it, and ask if the other (or others) are interested in joining you in some kind of mutual commitment to whatever list you jointly or collectively develop. If it works, you have a basis upon which to build. Perhaps you can use it as the foundation of the written house-rules contracts, that we will discuss later.

If it doesn't work, you might invite the other (or others) to read this book. Most people want to live in happy families, but many simply do not know how to go about it.

Occasionally a young person comes up against a stone wall in an effort like this. If so, all is not lost: this, too, is something we will investigate together in later chapters.

I Can't Trust You Anymore

Flo Capp walked into the local pub just in time to overhear a young woman say to Andy, "Tell me about yourself."

Before he had time to respond, his wife bellowed out, "Go and have a game of darts or something—*I'll do the telling!*"

And as he walked away, drink in hand, he mused, "All the world's a stage—and one of these days I might get the chance to play the lead in my own life."

There is a sense in which this is the story of adolescence: getting a chance to play the lead in your own life. It's nice to have a good coach standing in the wings to whom you can turn if prompting is needed, but most of us do not want someone sharing the spotlight with us on center stage, and coming up with the words when we're only pausing to take a breath.

Many parents are fearful of letting go. They're afraid their kids don't know the lines well enough *yet.* They force feed them with unsolicited advice beforehand, and interrogate them afterward, in an effort to make sure the show came off just right.

If a kid ad-libs or strays too far from the script, an anxious parent sometimes gets angry and blurts out, "I can't trust you anymore!" And you know what usually happens next: an ugly scene.

By the time a family gets around to consulting me with a problem like this, there is often another charge in the bill of particulars: lying! Of course kids lie. It's safer than answering an angry question with, "It's none of your business!"

At this point I encourage the parent (almost always one, not both) to examine what he or she means by, "I can't trust you anymore." There are times when this means, I can't trust you to keep your word. (And I addressed that issue in the last chapter where I suggested that we need to be careful about the agreements we make, lest we get the reputation for being undependable.) But I am usually told that it means, I can't trust you to do as you *should*! Upon further analysis it boils down to, I can't trust you to do as I say when you are out of my sight. Or perhaps simpler yet, I can't *control* you anymore.

Of course, young people resent this kind of surveillance and complete accountability to parents; I'm sure you would. It's like being boxed in with no elbow or leg room at all. And if we dig a bit deeper, we can usually find that the lack of trust springs from a deep-seated parental fear that he or she has not done enough to prepare the young person for life outside the home. Paradoxically, in most cases the parent has been overly conscientious, and needs to be reminded of all the positive dimensions of his or her parenting. So we discuss some of the young person's success stories.

Then we encourage the parent to let go of the fear and need to control, explaining that it will not work anyway. In fact, it will only alienate kids and cause them to become defiant. Parents can usually understand this and are open to being introduced to a better way, which can best be illustrated by this excerpt from a letter written by a mother to her daughter:

> I trust you! I do not want you to second-guess me, but to make the best decisions you can without interference from me.
>
> This way, when you make a mistake, I shall have no room to say, "I told you so!" And you'll have no reason to fear my displeasure. I still goof, and I don't expect you to do any better. My hope for both of us is that none of our mistakes will be so serious that they can't be repaired.

The daughter and I both thought this was a beautiful statement, and I share it here simply to let you know that there are constructive ways to structure relationships. And who knows, you might ask your mom or dad to read this, and then discuss it with you. If you can work it out between you, so much the better.

There is another subject that is closely related to trust, and that is ...

Lying

Just as, "I can't trust you anymore," usually means, *I can't control you anymore,* "You're lying," usually means something else, too.

Many parents assume that they have a right to be privy to everything that goes on in the minds and lives of their children: thoughts, feelings, information. If a question is asked, the truth, the whole truth, and nothing but the truth is anticipated. Gone is the right against self-incrimination; gone is the right to counsel. The parent acts as arresting officer, prosecutor, jury, judge, confinement officer, and probation officer. At least this is how it feels to you kids. And adults might be well advised to remember from their own youth just how overwhelming an experience it is to be intimidated and threatened by an adult.

"You're lying," might mean, *I suspect you're holding out on me,* or, *I don't believe you.* And to add insult to injury, instead of being presumed innocent until proven guilty, you are frequently presumed to be guilty until proven innocent. Furthermore, there is no appeal.

Is it any wonder, then, that under the stress of the moment a freaked-out kid blurts out a lie? Then he or she is immediately burdened with three things: guilt because of the lie; fear of being found out; and the need to remember the lie so that it doesn't get contradicted later.

There are, of course, specific reasons why young people lie. Some time ago, I made this list, and I was rather surprised to find that it was actually applicable to any age. Here it is:

1. To avoid punishment, humiliation, or ridicule;
2. To please another person by saying what one thinks he or she wants to hear;
3. To gain personal advantage;
4. To cover up a previous lie;
5. To protect another person;
6. To get another person in trouble;
7. To protect one's privacy;
8. To avoid a more lengthy explanation;
9. To eliminate a stressful situation.

In spite of the length of this list, that #7, "To protect one's privacy," is a big one. How many times would children, young people, and adults alike, love to respond to a personal question with a firm, "It's none of your business!" Instead of risking offending someone with honesty, we so easily lie. Little children know this; remember that grade school one-liner, "Ask me no questions, and I'll tell you no lies"?

So how do you stay true to yourself without having to resort to lying to your parents? Let's go back again to expectation #10:

> We will not lie to or otherwise deliberately deceive the other. This undermines trust, which is essential to our relationship. This does not mean that we are open to interrogation by the other, or that we are not entitled to privacy, including private thoughts—just that whatever we choose to express will always be the truth.

The concluding phrase is the key here. The following list suggests alternate responses to unwelcome questions from parents and others, allowing for both honesty and privacy.

Notice that, while each response can be an honest one, the privacy of the respondent is protected. Notice, too, the similarity of some of these responses and some of those mentioned in the chapter, *If You Love Me You Will*—where not hurting another person's feelings was also important. Ideally, for this to work best in a family all parties need to subscribe to the list of expectations and agree that it is okay to use such optional responses to questions. But in the absence of such an agreement, you can still use it solo to some extent.

1. "I'm not sure how to respond to that question; let me think it over and get back to you."
2. "It seems important for you to have that information; I'm not sure why."
3. "I'll be glad to answer that question if you'll let me rephrase it a bit."
4. "I have nothing to hide, and could answer that question; but for a number of reasons I don't think I should. I hope you can understand and accept that."
5. "If I answer that question, I'll be breaking a confidence with someone else. I'm sure you wouldn't want me to do that."
6. "If I answer that question, I'm afraid the information I give you may be used against me sometime."
7. "I'll eventually answer that question, but would rather not do it right now."
8. "When you ask a question like that, I feel like I'm in a courtroom."

If the members of your family can agree to accept the use of these responses, there should be no further need for lying by anyone! And if you have to go solo with it, I think you will find that the stronger your power base, the more likely you will be to have your responses accepted.

Let's look now at the matter of ...

Your Power Base

More or less, your power base has to do with what you are and have, what others think of you, and what you think of yourself. It determines whether people ignore you or listen to you when you speak; whether they trust you or not; whether they will follow you or not; whether they take you seriously or see you as a buffoon; whether or not they give you the benefit of the doubt in a tight situation; whether they like you or not.

A lot of things go into making up your power base: your age, health, appearance, educational level and record, job history, intelligence, marketable skills, extracurricular activities at school (sports, student government, school paper, clubs, etc.), community involvement, social connections, network of friends, attitudes toward alcohol–drugs–sex, and —yes—even the way you dress and part your hair. All of this is so whether or not we like it, and whether or not it is fair. Sometimes, of course, it can be very unfair—especially if you are a member of an identifiable minority group. Notice I did not include money and a car. This is because so many young people have found both to be more of a liability than an asset.

In my own youth there was a scout leader who frequently reminded us that on every day of our lives we were writing pages in a personal history that could never be erased or changed. It is this history that largely reveals what you have done about your power base, and gives the most accurate indication of what you will amount to in the days ahead. And if there's any doubt in your mind as to what it's like to live with little or no power base, look around you at those who sleep in doorways and carry around all their earthly possessions in a shopping cart.

Obviously, a good power base is a great asset in dealing with one's parents. Even if you are handicapped in some way—be it a physical, emotional or mental limitation, you can still have a strong power base, because what happens to us in life is not nearly as important as what *we choose* to do with those events and experiences.

So, if you want to get along better with your parents, develop your own power base; and remember, it's going to be with you for long after you're out on your own.

To put this in perspective, I touched on it here because the confidence that comes from having a strong power base will make it easier for you to utilize that list of alternative responses to help dodge parental interrogation. It will also demonstrate to your parents that you are indeed to be trusted. After all, who can argue with success?

To elaborate upon the importance of your network of friends, as it pertains to your power base, I'd like to tell you a story.

~ ~ ~

> A 28-year-old man returned home after completing 6 years of honorable military service. He planned to take 7 weeks to reconnect leisurely with loved ones and friends. This became, for the most part, a joyous experience.
>
> During his youth, he was so close to the parents of four of his friends that they more or less became surrogate parents. In each home he felt like a member of the family! He was always welcomed for a visit, a meal, or an overnight stay. No explanation was required.
>
> If for any reason he ever needed time, space or distance from a parent, he had a safe and respectable place to go. If his parents needed time alone away from home, they could leave town without worrying about him.

> High on the list of things he wanted to do upon his return was to spend some time with each of these four families. In three of the four homes it was a bittersweet experience, because during the previous year the fathers of the three boys had all died of cancer. He said, "It was as though I had lost my own father three times over."

~ ~ ~

For having relationships like these outside of his own home, he was most fortunate. And you will be too, if you can do likewise. It could even be with grandparents, or an aunt and uncle; but for best results it would be nice to have at least one family where you would find the welcome that my ex-sailor friend received—and for the same reasons.

Summary

When parents say, "I can't trust you anymore," they usually means they can't control you anymore. This kind of parental overcontrol frequently leads to lying on the part of kids. Children often lie for the same reasons adults do. The proposed model for responding to questions offers a way to be honest and to protect your privacy at the same time.

In looking at the nature and significance of a power base, we explored the importance of paying close attention to the development of yours, for it has a great deal to do with the amount of influence and credibility you have with others.

Your power base should never be used to intimidate others, or to get your way at someone else's expense. This is probably close to what Thomas Jefferson was talking about when he said that there is a *natural aristocracy* among people. Maybe this is what is referred to when one person says of another, "She has class!"

Rights, Duties, Privileges, Gratuities

Rights, duties, privileges and gratuities are all inescapably interconnected and interdependent. Let's look at them one or two at a time.

Rights and Duties

There is much confusion over the relationship between rights and duties. In fact, someone recently suggested, quite seriously, that our constitutional Bill of Rights should be followed by a Bill of Responsibilities. The point being that it may not be fair to grant rights all by themselves, without balancing them off with corresponding duties. We're going to focus now on how this works out in the family, and we'll begin by considering children's rights.

~ ~ ~

A divorced mother of three children remarried and invited her new husband and his son to move into her house, while the couple sold his house and settled on permanent arrangements. Her 15-year-old daughter then consulted an attorney to see how she could go about having the new stepfather evicted from *her* home. She felt that her rights had been violated.

~ ~ ~

A 17-year-old son insisted he had a right to use the family auto, and resisted having to justify each trip he wanted to make. If the car was in the driveway and he spoke first, he thought it should be his, no questions asked.

~ ~ ~

A 16-year-old girl was angry because she did not get $70 each month for clothing. She had a right to that much money in order to dress like her friends, she said.

~ ~ ~

A 22-year-old unemployed son thought he was entitled to $50 per week pocket money, in spite of the fact that his parents had a standing offer to pay him an hourly wage for outside grounds maintenance at their home.

~ ~ ~

On numerous occasions I have asked young people to make a list of their rights as family members. In other words, what did they think they had a right to expect from their parents? What did their folks owe them? I continue to be amazed at the diversity of those lists. You name it, and I've probably seen it on someone's list. I'm not talking about that list of expectations we looked at earlier; I'm talking about what some kids see to be their inalienable rights!

I have also asked parents to make lists of what they consider to be their kids' rights. That is, what are their duties toward the children? The strange thing is that on occasions too frequent to mention, the lists of parents and children have not been that far apart.

~ ~ ~

One night the evening news reported a case where a young man brought suit against his parents in an attempt to force them to pay for his college education. The court ruled against the son.

Another night, they reported a case where parents had established an educational fund for their son early in life, which was supposed to provide enough for 4 years of tuition, books, room, board, and transportation at a state university. After completing high school he decided that he wanted to attend an expensive private college. I guess his parents believed that they owed it to him, because it was reported that they refinanced their home in order to make possible his dream.

~ ~ ~

A professional man with a limiting physical handicap was ready for retirement, but decided to buy his daughter a $100,000 condominium so that he wouldn't have to worry about her in his old age. Now he can't afford to retire, and might not live until old age.

~ ~ ~

I mention these stories only to illustrate the importance of young people and their parents addressing these issues early, in order to avoid the unhappy conflict that can take place later. If you have not yet experienced difficulty here, you're lucky. But it might still be worthwhile for you to go over this chapter carefully, so as to be better prepared if conflict on this subject should arise in the future.

I'd like to ask you to do something now: divide a sheet of paper into two columns. In the left column make a list of your rights; in the right-hand space, list all the privileges you have, either things you are permitted to do for yourself or things your parents do for you. Take some time with this and think it over.

Next, try to imagine yourself arguing your case before a juvenile court judge. You are complaining that your parents have violated one or more of your rights, which you want restored and enforced. Will the judge rule in your favor, or laugh at you?

I have gone through a parental version of this exercise with a number of groups, and it has always been an eye-opener for most participants. Without exception, after a spirited discussion between those parents present, a lot of *rights* were moved over into the right-hand column. Eventually the list of children's rights consistently boiled down to six: food, shelter, clothing, health care, public education through high school, and love. Sounds pretty Spartan, doesn't it? What about all the other goodies that most kids enjoy and think they have coming? They are *all* privileges, lovingly bestowed as time, energy, and resources permit—and for as long as kids deserve and appreciate them!

It is a startling idea to most young people that they should have to earn and appreciate so many of the things that they have taken for granted! The following comments have been made by parents, with a great deal of relief—and even laughter, as they have contemplated the implications of that list of six basic rights for kids:

> "As long as meals are nourishing, I guess I don't owe it to anyone to buy expensive boxes of cold cereal or prepared foods, do I? I can even go vegetarian once in awhile."

> "You mean I'm not bad or wrong to insist on taking the kids shopping for clothing at the Salvation Army Thrift Store?"

> "If what you other parents are saying is true, my boys do not have a right to separate bedrooms. As much as we'd like to accommodate them on that subject, we flat can't afford a larger home right now."

> "You're absolutely right! There are other ways for our children to get a college education than for us to go into hock for the whole thing."

> "Because I love my children, I have to be concerned with the quality of our family life. It's not fair to any of us if their father and I bust our backs to earn more money just so we can give them more things."

> "I'm glad my daughter has someone to love her; otherwise her world would be a cold and lonely place. Without the ingredient of love, the other five rights wouldn't mean much."

Love is the right of all people, and if you'd like some idea of how lonely it can be without love, you have only to recall the stark look on the dirty faces of the abandoned children in Romanian orphanages that we all saw on television in 1990.

So you see—your legitimate rights become, in a sense, your parents' duties. But there's more: these duties are enforceable. There are numerous cases where children have been taken away from their parents because of abuse or neglect. And furthermore, the state has the expectation that your parents will raise you in such a way that you will amount to something and not get into trouble with the law, or otherwise become a burden on society. They don't tell your parents how to pull this off; that is left up to them. And it ain't easy. Public education by itself will not guarantee it. All the parental love in the world will not guarantee it. But the state expects the parents to do their best to raise responsible kids.

More and more, parents are being held accountable in court for any delinquent behavior exhibited by their children. Unless! Unless they see it coming and call for help *before* a kid gets into serious trouble.

Sometime I'm going to give a talk to a parents' group on the subject of how to raise responsible kids. It will consist of these points (if you like them, pass them on):

1. Set a clear example of responsible adult behavior.
2. Don't take on the responsibilities of others.
3. Don't shield your kids from the consequences of their own behavior; that is how they learn.
4. Be there for your kids when they need you.
5. If you see one of them headed for trouble, don't be afraid to say so; but always request permission first! And if you have a suggestion to make, present it as a possible option. Better yet, give at least two options. This will minimize any guilt one might feel for not following what looks like advice when only one option is offered.

6. Provide a loving, realistic and enforceable structure for your children that will reflect your values. That structure should define the limits of acceptable behavior, otherwise the family can easily deteriorate into a mere collection of competing people.
7. Remember, like parents, kids *are* anxious to please. Recent research has shown that family ties are far more important to young people than peer relationships in shaping behavior.

That idea of punishing parents for the screwups of their kids is not a bad deal, is it? The children have the rights and the parents have the duties—both to the kids and to the state. All the youngster has to say is, "Hey Dad, back off or I'll throw a brick through the principal's window and you'll go to the slammer!" Right? Wrong, because there's a catch. Parents also have rights, and kids also have enforceable duties. There's no such thing as a free lunch; it's a two-way street.

Typically, parents don't seem to have as great a tolerance for anarchy as do kids. To prevent anarchy there must be a structure. Structures limit freedom by setting limits and establishing rules. The more kids there are in a family, the more rules are needed—up to a point. This doesn't leave much room for the free spirit who says, "Hey man, I gotta be me; don't fence me in with a bunch of restrictions!" If you know *any* person who says there are no rules in his or her family, don't you believe it. They may not be written down, but they are there!

In the Commonwealth of Massachusetts, my home state, parents are expected to establish rules that are *reasonable and fair*, and their children are expected to live by them. If a young person chronically ignores the rules, there is an *or else* factored in: a parent can file a *CHINS Petition* (Child In Need of Services), and the juvenile court system will swing into action and engage in what someone has called *an attitude adjustment program.* This can, if serious enough, include removal of the child from the home temporarily or permanently. (Many other states have similar provisions.)

Since no one likes rules, it's easy to understand why kids might tend to resist them. If you are one of those who fears rules, here are a few things to keep in mind:

1. Written rules are much better than verbal ones: they are clear and less likely to be misunderstood or forgotten. Given a choice, go for a written code.
2. Rules that apply to both parents and children will be accepted better than those aimed only at children. Where appropriate, therefore, ask your parents to avoid a double standard.
3. Some house rules only reflect state and local laws over which parents have no control. As such, they are not arbitrary (i.e. drug and alcohol prohibitions).
4. Some house rules exist because of a legal requirement for parents to exercise some measure of control over what goes on in the home. For example, there is no way a parent can be responsible for what goes on in the house if, in his or her absence, a bunch of kids are permitted to come in for a party.
5. Some rules may be an expression of ownership. For example, does a mother not have a right to be upset if her daughter borrows her clothes without permission, or a father to be annoyed if his drill is missing the next time he wants to use it?
6. Some house rules may reflect an awareness of health, safety, and sanitation requirements.
7. Some rules are designed to protect property.

8. Some rules show a desire to cooperate with the schools, as in the establishment of a quiet time for study and homework.

More could be said on the subject, but perhaps this is enough to illustrate the point that some rules are unavoidable, and that they are not necessarily the product of a fiendish mind set on creating as much discomfort as possible for kids.

Now let's move from theory to practice. On many occasions I have helped fractured families to get organized and back on track. If the family is in some kind of crisis, that will need to be dealt with first, but once that brush fire is extinguished, we try to focus upon the dysfunctional elements in the system. At some point I usually ask the parents to do some homework in the area of rules: specifically, to write down a list of their own *nonnegotiable* house rules; later on, we include the children in an exercise to develop the negotiable ones. (These are the ones that include such things as curfew, allowance, chore distribution, and any special needs.)

Once this basic list is completed and polished, we have a family session where the parents present their list. It is not even open to discussion. It's take it or leave it; and the *or else's* are clearly stated. This will sound like hype, but there is only one response I have ever seen from kids to this kind of presentation: a sigh of relief! The children knew what their parents were up to, and they feared the worst. Besides, I have yet to see the young person who did not want a structure of some kind. To have no reference point for behavior can be overwhelming, and children have a right to resent not having one. In some cases I think the message a difficult kid may be trying to send is that if parents don't care enough to set some limits, there is no end to the unacceptable behavior he is capable of!

It is unrealistic to expect one person's set of house rules to be applicable to all others, because there are simply too many variables from one family to another. Nevertheless, I shall share a typical one for illustrative purposes, and then discuss it. A real value in something like this is that it is always easier to modify someone else's list than to start from scratch with a blank sheet of paper and draw up one's own. This particular set of rules was designed for a family consisting of mother, father, 17-year-old son, and 11- and 7-year-old daughters. I have included the full document, including an introduction. A closing paragraph appears at the end of the next section.

House Rules

These rules are set forth unilaterally because we, as parents, feel morally and legally responsible for providing a structure for our family. The only other alternative is chaos. And the larger the family, the more important it becomes to have some sort of structure. This list specifically expands upon, but does not replace the list of our expectations which you have already received.

We feel that the following rules are reasonable and fair. They should not limit true freedom, but rather should promote, facilitate, and enhance it.

These rules are seen by us as being non-negotiable, and binding until modified. We may, as a family, develop additional rules, but they will be negotiated between all of us. (Examples: curfew, distribution of chores, use of family auto, amount of allowance, pay for housework, etc.)

You will notice that we expect to live by many of these rules ourselves, where they are applicable. We want to practice what we preach, and do not believe in a double standard.

Should you wish to add to this list or prepare one of your own which identifies your expectations for us, we are open to such a possibility. If you are interested, let's talk about it.

If the time comes when you decide to reject one or more of these rules, we expect that you will say so, thus giving us an opportunity to deal openly and lovingly with our conflict, in an attempt to resolve it constructively. A stalemate will result in our seeking professional help, since we are committed to you and to win-win solutions to all our conflicts.

1. Physical violence (including retaliation and escalation of conflict) is completely unacceptable on the part of any of us. Force may be used to protect one's self or another, but may not be used punitively or in anger.

2. When anyone leaves the house, a signout board will be used which will indicate destination and estimated time of return. If we change an itinerary, a clear trail will be left so that we can be found in case of emergency. More than a 30-minute delay in arrival time will be reported in advance by telephone, if possible, or as soon as convenient in the event an emergency prevents us from doing so in advance.

3. Deliberate destruction of property will not be tolerated under any circumstances; neither will any behavior be tolerated which can reasonably be expected to result in destruction of property.

4. Children will be provided with a personal allowance, the amount and scope of which

will be negotiated. There are no strings attached to this; it is not compensation for chores. If children are willing to work to *earn* extra money, there will probably be seasonal or occasional tasks available that are not in the category of routine chores.

5. All members of the family are expected to share in the chores necessary to maintain the household. Each one's individual responsibilities will be a matter for us to negotiate, but no one will be expected to have a disproportionate share of unpleasant tasks.
6. Privacy, private space and property will not be violated by any of us, for any reason (i.e. closed doors, mail, diaries, telephone conversations, wallets and purses, clothing, records and tapes, and so forth).
7. Shared space will be kept shipshape at all times, with the user restoring it to its normal state following use. Only in personal space (i.e. a bedroom that is not shared) will clutter be permitted. *Clutter* is not meant to include anything that is unsafe, potentially destructive of property, or unsanitary.
8. When an adult is not present, friends may not enter the house except in emergency, or with prior parental consent.
9. As long as there is only one telephone in the house, incoming and outgoing calls will be limited to 10 minutes, with a minimum of 10 minutes between calls, so as to allow time to receive incoming calls. When *both* parents are home, this rule may be relaxed upon

request. Consideration will be given to authorizing children to have their own telephone when they are able to pay for it.

10. Children are responsible for establishing their own times for retiring and rising, getting themselves to work or school on time and completing their own laundry (unless we negotiate differently). They will not be bugged by us on these issues.

11. We will negotiate a time for breakfast and dinner, and it is expected that we will share these meals together, unless an absence is negotiated in advance.

12. A quiet time will be observed each evening, Sunday through Thursday, the duration of which will be negotiated. During this time, there will be no television or telephone use, except with special permission, thus providing an atmosphere conducive to study, homework, reading, and so forth.

13. No illegal activity will be tolerated in or outside of the home. This includes possession and/or use of illicit drugs or alcohol.

14. A polite no smoking sign is posted at the entrance to our home. We expect all family members and visitors to honor this request.

15. Deliberate deception will not be tolerated. This undermines trust, which is essential to any quality relationship. This does not mean that we are free to interrogate each other, or to invade each other's privacy (including private thoughts), just that whatever we choose to express shall always be the truth. (Same as Expectation #10)

So much for all but the final paragraph, which will be discussed later. Now, how does a parent enforce these rules? Yell and scream? No. Threaten and get ugly? No. To understand the leverage parents have for enforcement, let's move on to the next section ...

Privileges

Go back to your list of rights and privileges. What did you place in the right-hand column? Would you like to compare your choices with a composite list that parents and young people have helped me to collect? Here it is:

1. Use of household appliances and equipment, including, but not limited to, radio, stereo, TV, VCR, sewing machine, tools, family auto, sports and athletic items, office machines, telephone;
2. Access to facilities of organizations in which parents may hold memberships: social clubs, community centers, athletic organizations (ski club, swim club, rod and gun club, YMCA, etc.);
3. Use of any equipment you may have in your room, regardless of who paid for it, including your radio, stereo, TV and computer;
4. Membership and/or participation in social, athletic, cultural or recreational activities, whether school related or not;
5. Group or private instruction in music (instrumental or vocal), dance, swimming, karate, art (of all types);
6. Entertaining friends at home, including overnight visits;
7. Vacations, travel, summer camp, family outings.

Quite a list, isn't it? Most young people would see just about all of the above items as rights. It's only when a kid screws up and gets grounded that he or she finds out just how few enforceable rights there really are. This brings us back to the list of house rules. Here is the final paragraph that was omitted earlier. It would be included in the actual document, and is only one paragraph.

> *You enjoy a number of privileges and benefits as a member of this family, in addition to your basic rights. Please be advised that deliberate or repeated violations of the above rules will be met with suspension of one or more privileges. In other words, we will trade off the privileges we give* ***you*** *for the cooperation you give* ***us****. When you become self-supporting and live on your own, you will be free to do as you please. In the meantime, please remember the Golden Rule,* ***Whoever has the gold, makes the rules****.*

A parent said, "That's the way it is in real life; why should it be otherwise in our home?" Another said, "You have no idea what written rules did for our family. Before that I was going crazy defending, explaining and justifying my every decision to the kids." These parents were obviously happier with rules clearly spelled out and written down, and I'll tell you something, when you have happy parents, the entire family is better off.

These rules and privileges also provide a rational structure for a parent to deal with his or her own behavior, as well as yours. Too often, tension and pressure build up in a parent until there is an explosion, and an ugly, sweeping condemnation and grounding. Then the parent has to either back off (and risk losing face), or enforce a bad decision that hurts everyone.

With this list, the specific violation can be identified. If discussion and a gentle reminder don't work, then the parent has a wide range of privileges from which to choose, if a suspension seems appropriate. The whole purpose of this is only to obtain compliance. It's a way of saying, "If you insist on doing such and such, why should I continue to play Santa Claus and carry on business as usual? This action will serve to remind you of what we expect." Is this punishment? Technically, yes; but I prefer to think of it simply as the suspension of a privilege. It sounds better.

Let's look at some real-life stories that illustrate how all this can work.

~ ~ ~

> Three young children of a divorced mother, and two children of a father who was also divorced, were all brought together under one roof by the remarriage of their parents. I met regularly with the seven of them in a long effort to help make their new stepfamily function smoothly and efficiently.
>
> We had moved beyond the house-rules stage and had successfully worked through the identification and distribution of chores. There was only one problem: when the parents arrived home from work, the chores were not completed. What were the kids doing? Watching television, of course, each waiting for the others to start his or her chores. Maybe they lost track of time. Nothing malicious, I am sure. Occasionally, a few or even most of the chores were done, but never all of them. Frequently, a crucial step in dinner preparation was omitted, like forgetting to take a casserole out of the refrigerator and put it into the oven.
>
> The parents were understandably discouraged, and were not sure just how to get a handle on the situation. I suggested that they purchase an automobile ignition switch and have it installed in the TV chassis. They did, and it worked like this: the last parent out in the morning locked the TV; the first one home in the evening unlocked it—if *all* the chores were done. If only one kid's chores were not completed, the TV still remained off. Of course, the other children thought it was unfair for all of them to be inconvenienced because of the negligence of only one. The

parents almost fell for this, but I urged them to stay with the program and to let the kids work out the details between themselves.

For two more nights, the parents were met with, "We all did our chores, but Charlie (or whoever the obstructionist was) didn't do his."

The parents responded with, "That's your problem; don't bug us. The TV goes on when *all* the chores are done." or words to that effect.

Neither the parents nor I know what went on behind the scene, but on the third evening all the chores were completed before Mom and Dad arrived. And that's the way it was every evening after that.

~ ~ ~

A 16-year-old boy insisted on falling asleep with the stereo playing next to the wall that separated his bedroom from his parents'. Sometimes the parents didn't realize that it was on until they climbed into bed and stopped talking. Then the steady booming kept his mother awake. She in turn would ask her husband to go in and turn it off, since his side of the bed was closest to the door. So it became a real pain to both of them.

Concluding that the son was simply indifferent to their needs, the father made one more clear and polite statement about how unacceptable the son's behavior was. That night, instead of turning off the stereo, the father unplugged it and cut off the plug.

When the son discovered this, he was outraged that his property had been *destroyed*, and threatened to blow the whistle on his father to the psychiatrist the three of them were seeing. At their next family therapy session, the son confidently told of this blatant violation of his rights. The therapist quietly replied, "You're lucky I'm not your father; I would have taken a sledge hammer to your stereo." One week later, a new plug was placed on the wire, and the son learned to turn off his stereo.

~ ~ ~

A 14-year-old girl verbally abused her mother more than anyone her age I had ever seen. Since her father was a long-distance truck driver, the mother was on her own during the week. The mother finally had enough, and said she was ready to do whatever it took to silence her daughter. During our discussion, I learned that the daughter's most cherished privilege was use of the telephone. Since the phone had a rotary dial, I suggested that she stop at a stationary store on the way home and purchase a lock that I knew was available to secure telephones against unauthorized use. She installed it and waited.

The daughter exploded, demanding to know what happened. Her mother calmly delivered a well-rehearsed speech, "Sally, the telephone is locked because of the way you talked to me this morning. The lock will remain in place for 24 hours, to remind you not to (here she raised her voice) *ever, ever* talk to me that way again! And if you should do it again, the phone will remain locked for at least 7 days."

The girl was so subdued the next time I saw her that I thought she had had a lobotomy.

~ ~ ~

Parents were so disgusted with the condition of their son's room that they stripped it of everything except an air mattress, a sleeping bag, a pillow, a table, a chair and a lamp. He had to earn back everything else—piece by piece.

~ ~ ~

A father, whose son was in constant conflict with him over use of the family car, designed a car-use-request form which had to be filled in and submitted to him at least 24 hours in advance of any intended use.

Information to be supplied included: date, destination, distance, itinerary, passengers, departure and return times, purpose of trip and telephone number at each destination.

Then there was a statement the son had to sign to the effect that alcohol would not be carried or consumed in the car; he would fill the tank with gasoline before returning home; he understood that any violation would result in the indefinite suspension of his driving privileges; all his passengers had permission from their parents to ride with him; he would not get upset if his parents were unable to grant his request because of their personal plans.

By the time the son completed one of these forms, it was pretty obvious that his use of the family car was a real privilege and not a right—and he began to act accordingly.

~ ~ ~

I could share some more stories, but I think perhaps the point is clear. What I wanted to show was that:

1. The parents did not have to get ugly or abusive.
2. The parents suspended or set limits on a privilege as an attention getter, to protect themselves and to effect compliance with the rules.
3. The parents gained credibility, and probably some respect, in the process.
4. The family experienced a greater measure of harmony.
5. The whole process was very clear. No misunderstanding here about what was going on, or about what was expected.

Among the negotiable agreements families have to work out is the distribution of chores. I have found that family members are much more compliant and cooperative if they have shared in the decisions about who does what. No one seems to mind an unpleasant task or two, as long as other family members also have an equal number of them, and as long as the unpleasant ones are rotated periodically among all family members.

With all this material about rights, duties and privileges, there is one thing that can never be legislated, and that is the attitude you take toward it all. One cannot pretend to have a good attitude just because it pays off; but if one does think and feel positively, it will certainly pay off in innumerable ways. And that brings us to the last section of this chapter ...

Gratuities

Isn't a gratuity a tip you leave, or a bonus, or a gift by which you express pleasure to another person in some way? My dictionary describes it as *something given without claim or demand.* Examples are birthday, anniversary or holiday gifts.

Maybe some of the items on the list of privileges we discussed earlier are more appropriately considered gratuities, but I'll let that list stand and start a new one of things that are clearly in the area of gratuities. Take a look at some of the things parents do for their kids when they really like them:

1. Parents spend time with their kids—above and beyond the call of duty.
2. Parents talk their kids up to others, and obviously take pride and find pleasure in their kids and their kids achievements.
3. Parents keep photo albums and scrapbooks on their kids.
4. Parents get involved in and support the programs their kids are participating in.
5. If they can afford it, parents let their kids participate in a wide range of educational, recreational and cultural extracurricular activities.
6. A parents' home is open to their kids' friends; so much so that the friends get to know and like the parents.
7. Parents let their kids bring friends along on some family outings and vacations.

8. Parents do their best to help kids with further education beyond high school.

There is no end to the good things that can come your way when you are on good terms with Mom and Dad. They are, hopefully, the ones who will always be there for you, no matter what. That kind of relationship is certainly a worthwhile prize—for all of us.

If you want to look beyond that, there is still more. If you are a daughter, your folks will want to provide you with as nice a wedding as is practical. And when your first child is born, Mom will be there with you. After that, there will be two sets of grandparents conspiring to spoil your children, which is essentially what being a grandparent is all about.

If there is any way they can afford to, they will want to help you when it comes time to buy your first home. Friends recently tried to sell their home in our neighborhood. They told us that at least 80 percent of the inquiries they received were from parents who were looking for something affordable for their children.

In other words, there is something very special and basic about family. Success stories are no accident; they come about only as a result of hard work on the part of both kids *and* their parents.

Contrast this scenario, though, with a true story about a father and mother who invited their 17-year-old son to accompany them on a vacation trip out west. They were driving through a very sparsely populated desert area, in a rented car, when they spotted a small service station ahead. The son wanted to use the restroom, so they stopped. When he returned, the parents and the car were nowhere to be seen. Confused, he asked the proprietor where they were. "Oh," he said, "that last car? I don't know, but they asked me to give you this." It was an envelope with a hundred dollar bill enclosed, together with a card on which was written this brief note, *Good luck! If you care to, please look us up—after you have grown up.*

Whatever the story behind something like this, it is always very sad. And for every kid who gets evicted, there are probably at least a few others who see it coming and beat the parents to it by just disappearing, rarely to be heard from again. Something needs to be said about this, and I have purposely waited until now to say it.

In that list of rights you will notice that there is a consensus among parents that kids are entitled to shelter. Not necessarily living in the family home, but *shelter.* This can be interpreted by different people to mean different things. Once parents think about it seriously, they usually give up on the notion that a youngster has a right to live in the family home, no matter what. Increasingly, they tend to see it as a privilege, which, like all privileges, can be suspended or withdrawn. Call it what you will: eviction, emancipation, being kicked out or whatever; parents *can* do it, and do it legally! To put *living at home* in any formal list of privileges might sound menacing; that is why I left it out until now—just as a reminder that losing it *is* a distinct possibility.

An attorney friend tells me that there is no court in the land that would compel parents to keep an unwanted child at home. If the child is below a certain age, the state might expect the parents to contribute toward his or her maintenance; but in such a case, parents might consider it a small price to pay to get rid of what they see as a headache. If you remember all of this, it could help you to avoid a catastrophe.

Summary

I hope you can see from this chapter that a fair and workable structure in your family is infinitely better for you than the anarchy that exists in some homes. You have learned to distinguish between your rights and your privileges. You have given some thought to the nature of your parents' rights, as well as your own. And you have considered what you are willing to give in exchange for all the privileges you have now, and expect to receive in the future.

If you think the system described here is an improvement over what exists in your family, don't hesitate to invite your parents to read this material (if yours is not already a joint effort with your parents) and then discuss it with you. Too many parents are too busy and too proud to get involved with preventive maintenance. They tend to wait until there is trouble and then ask a counselor to help them straighten things out.

When Parents Part Ways

With all the fine books that have been published on the subject of divorce, one might wonder why I discuss it at all in this volume. I can certainly not do it justice in any comprehensive sort of way, but since we are focusing on understanding and getting along with parents, we can hardly afford to avoid the subject altogether, especially when the divorce rate is so high.

Experts used to think that children were resilient enough to bounce right back from a divorce with little more than short-term pain and inconvenience. The research results beginning to come in now suggest quite the opposite. Unless one has actually experienced a divorce, there is no way he or she can readily understand what it does to a person. So perhaps it's not surprising that we have underestimated its impact on children as well.

An out-of-town rabbi lectured locally on this subject a few years ago and made this observation, "The only time a nice friendly divorce is even possible is when there are no children and each spouse has found another partner."

I have talked with many unfortunate persons who have experienced both the death of a spouse *and* divorce. Without exception, every one said that divorce was by far the more difficult of the two.

At least once each week someone in the process of divorce says to me, "Now that that issue is over with, I am sure that the worst is behind me." And always, he or she finds out that the worst is yet to come! In other words, divorce, like a severe earthquake, is an unimaginably devastating experience, the aftershocks of which continue to be felt for years to come. So how can you kids not be affected, also—for years to come?

A fear of how divorce will affect the children causes some parents—who knows how many—to stay together *for the sake of the kids.* This is always a high-risk decision at best, because it usually only postpones the inevitable; and at worst, it can be harder on the kids than a divorce. This dilemma may be the reason I have never known a parent who jumped impulsively into a divorce action. My experience suggests that a decision by one or both parents to terminate a marriage comes only after much agony over the risks and possible benefits to all concerned—especially the kids!

Friends, relatives and well-intentioned people-helpers frequently lean real hard on parents to *think of the children* when considering divorce. They forget too easily that it is often consideration for the kids that tips the scales toward a decision to call it quits.

The Humpty Dumpty Syndrome *is* a reality. This, of course, is where "... all the king's horses and all the king's men ..." can't put Humpty Dumpty back together again—or a happy family, either.

There can come a time when children, and other loved ones, are well advised to try to accept—as gracefully as possible—the decision to end a marriage. For children, this is no time to question seriously the devotion of one's parents, although I recognize that at times it is difficult not to do so.

If your parents ever split up, try to believe the best about both of them. This means resisting the temptation to take sides: something no parent should ever encourage you to do anyway. Neither parent is divorcing you; they are divorcing each other! They are the only parents you will ever have, and no one can or should ever want to take the place of either one of them in your life. There are some significant exceptions, but in most cases there is no reason why a child cannot continue to have a high quality relationship with both parents after the dust settles.

In addition, I have seen case after case where the quality of the relationship between kids and their parents has gone up appreciably following divorce. And this is not surprising, since parents can hardly be at their best with the kids, when their marriage is coming apart at the seams. They have to focus so much energy on just keeping their heads above water (including going to work every day) that they are often emotionally drained and physically exhausted virtually all the time. Hold that clearly in mind, and it may help you to keep a level head when it looks as if your parents are losing theirs.

When there is talk of divorce, children are often overwhelmed by confusing and conflicting emotions. Some try to deny it, refusing to face or discuss it, at least for a time. It is not uncommon for children to blame themselves for the breakup, and then try their best to undo the imagined damage by pushing for a reconciliation. This is one of those times when it can be very tempting to push a parent's fear, pity, duty, or guilt button with the if-you-love-me routine. And high on any list of feelings must be those of fear, anxiety, uncertainty, and powerlessness, as kids wonder what in the world is going to happen to them after the court has made its decision.

Courts are doing their very best these days to make the divorce process as humane as possible. With the introduction of no-fault divorce, a big step has already been taken in this direction.

Of the many divorce proceedings I have witnessed, I was especially pleased with how one probate judge routinely opened his custody hearings. It went like this: "Let's see—Counselor, you represent the wife. And Counselor," pointing toward the other attorney, "you represent the husband, don't you? And who, may I ask, represents the children here?" There was always a long pause at this point. "Come on; who represents the interests of the minor children of these divorcing parents?" There was generally another long pause, during which an expectant hush fell over the courtroom, before the judge spoke again, "So, no one, I see! Well, let me tell you this, that's *my* job here today! *I'm* here to represent the interests of the children. Anyone have a problem with that?" After more silence, he said, "Good!" and proceeded with the hearing.

I would not be surprised if at some point in the not-too-distant future an attorney is actually appointed to represent all minor children in custody hearings. Not just in custody disputes, but in all custody hearings. I don't think we are far from such a position in Massachusetts, for the court already takes a very close look at custody agreements worked out by parents in advance of the hearing, to make sure that the rights and interests of children are protected. Of course, when there is an unresolved dispute between parents, whether it involves custody or not, it is customary for a representative of the court to investigate the case and either try to mediate the disagreement or make recommendations to the court.

I do not suggest that the children necessarily know what resolution is appropriate in a custody case, but I do believe their opinions should be paid heed. When they are ignored, it adds to their feeling of powerlessness and helplessness. It also reduces them to a position where it may look as though they are being treated more as property than as persons.

All children, including you, have legitimate rights and interests in what happens in a divorce proceeding. You should not be treated as a mindless pawn. And even after a decision has been rendered by the court, it is never set in concrete. If it doesn't work out as expected, it is always subject to review and redefinition. I have heard judges repeatedly explain this to parents, since they want it remembered that it is the court that has final say in matters of custody and support.

How do you exercise this right? Well, the best place to begin is with your parents. Stay informed, ask questions, give opinions and input on matters that affect you. Talk to their attorneys. And if necessary, go to the probation office of the probate court, and you will be directed to someone who will listen to you. Hopefully, your questions will be answered and your input valued.

Custody decisions are rarely easy, since there are many more options than meet the eye. I once made a list of all I could think of, and identified thirteen for situations where there is only one child. With two or more children, the variations increase significantly. In most cases, however, they number about five.

Although you should get involved, to some extent, in your parents' divorce, you should be careful not to become over-involved to the point of taking sides with one parent against the other. Young people place themselves at risk if they become a confidant or a buddy to a divorcing parent.

On many, many occasions a mother has been awarded physical custody of a teenaged son, who continues to live with her in what used to be the family home. Without realizing the danger, the mother may permit or encourage him to become the man of the house, moving into whatever vacuum is left by the father's departure. She confides in him, goes out socially with him as her escort, and eventually finds that she must account to him for what she does with her time—including dating, when she is ready for it. I have seen women who have chosen to keep a romantic involvement secret until the possessive son leaves home. Boys—watch out for this; it can be very, very risky. Your mother is quite vulnerable at this point in her life, and you will best serve her interests (and yours) if you continue to be her *son*!

Girls—you face a similar risk, only more complicated. If you become the lady of the house for your father, there will probably be some mothering responsibility you accept toward younger siblings, thus laying the foundation for an intense rivalry with any woman who even remotely looks like a potential stepmother. And with mother, there is not only the problem of a confidant role, but of acting toward her more as a sister than as a daughter. Therefore, you too will best serve your parents interests (and yours) if you continue to be their *daughter.*

To both daughters and sons I suggest, at the first mention of the word *divorce,* head for the nearest school guidance counselor, psychologist or social worker to find out where you can connect with a support group for children of separating and divorcing parents. Chances are there may even be one in your own school. You should not go through this alone: it has the power to make you physically ill, scramble your thinking, and put you hopelessly behind in your studies. Absolutely one of the worst things you can do is to isolate yourself, however noble and considerate it may sound. Divorce does not have to be the end of the world, for either your parents or for you. There is life after divorce, and a good support group can help you to cling to that hope and to find that life.

This is very sober and heavy stuff: no laughs here. Sorry, but that's the way it is. Also, this material needs to be somewhat more technical than most of what we've been discussing thus far, due to it's nature. So you may want to take a breather about now, to clear your head before continuing on with the problem of ...

A Stranger In the House

The Second Time Around—It has been said that getting married for the second time represents a triumph of hope over experience. Whatever it means, most divorced persons remarry within 2 years. And many of them will divorce for the second time, with the most frequently given reason being conflict between spouses over children and conflict between stepparent and stepchildren.

One would think that adults would do better the second time around, having learned from experience, feeling more mature this time, knowing what it's like to be a single parent, and so forth. But it doesn't always work that way.

Some newly re-marrieds discover too late that they chose a second partner who turned out to be remarkably like the first. Others discover, also too late, that they placed too much emphasis upon selecting a new partner who was dramatically different from the first, without stopping to consider how they themselves might have contributed to the breakup of the first marriage.

Not very good odds, are they? Maybe you have a right to get scared when you see Mom or Dad getting romantically involved again. The temptation is great, at this point, for young people to engage in passive aggressive behaviors calculated to scare off the would-be stranger in the house. And it sometimes works, even though it is sure to be very upsetting to the parent, who understandably feels that the kids were just too possessive and selfish to share him or her with a new partner. So what do you do? You don't have too many constructive options, but I think there is something you can do. First, let me share a story …

~ ~ ~

The Case for Premarital Counseling—I worked with a man I shall call Tom over the course of about 18 months, toward the end of which time he separated from and initiated divorce action against his now ex-wife. There were no children. Still, the loss of his marriage was understandably difficult, especially since he was a clergyman and had no idea how his congregation would react. It turned out that the church handled it well, and a few months after the divorce our sessions were suspended by mutual consent.

Following a respectful period of time, he became increasingly involved with a divorced mother of two children. When he told me his good news, I said something about hoping he would seek premarital counseling soon. Our paths crossed several times thereafter, and each time he dodged the issue I had raised.

One day I pressed him on the subject, and he asked why. I replied, "Tom, if a couple came to you professionally and asked you to officiate at their marriage, what would you say?"

"Yes," was his immediate response; and he continued, "but first you'll have to see me for a series of premarital counseling sessions."

I didn't see how he could have walked into that one, and asked why he thought his situation was any different. He exclaimed, "Because we've already decided that we want to be married!"

I patiently explained what I erroneously thought had been obvious: that premarital counseling is rarely designed to help couples decide whether or not to get married. Much more often its purpose is to help couples get off to a good start, to enhance their understanding of each other, to facilitate good communication between them, and to help them face and deal with some important issues they might have unintentionally avoided—like dealing with stepchildren. That seemed to be a new thought to him.

Since I had worked with him during the dissolution of his first marriage, I referred him to another therapist for additional joint work with his fiancee. It was a great experience for them, and they are still happily married—in spite of his two stepchildren that his wife brought with her, and three additional children subsequently born to them.

~ ~ ~

Over the course of my career I have worked with many, many people in the process of divorce. When we are about to part ways, one of the final subjects I *always* address is the value and importance of premarital counseling. And yet very few have followed my advice on the subject, even though they trusted me enough to seek me out for the second time, when the new marriage was in trouble.

Perhaps, like Tom, folks are afraid their therapist is going to try to talk them out of getting married. Granted, some couples in premarital counseling decide to put off their wedding, either temporarily or permanently, but that is always their decision.

Why do I tell you this story? First, to let you know that premarital counseling is not yet the *in* thing. Hopefully, it may be some day; I understand in California anyone below the age of 21 applying for a marriage license must give evidence of having attended a prescribed number of sessions with a state certified marriage and family therapist. And secondly, to give you some ammunition to use with your mom or dad when either of them starts looking and sounding romantic. Tell your parent about any fears and anxieties you may have and, as a condition of your unqualified support for anything serious, suggest that he or she get premarital counseling from a licensed or certified professional. And ask that at some point you be included in the process, too! Remember, without this, the chances for success in a second marriage are less than you get with the flip of a coin.

I think this is something you can safely push. After all, if your parent doesn't like it, to whom can he or she complain? For your sake, I hope your mom or dad doesn't respond by coming home some day and abruptly saying, "Surprise—guess what? We're married!" That is simply *too* much! Under such circumstances you would have a right to feel violated.

Help For Yourself—If this sort of thing should happen to you, and you need help in handling the situation, to whom can you turn? Is there anyone, or do you just have to suffer in silence? During my final session with every family or couple I work with, I always ask them to agree that if any family member wants professional help to deal with a problem, it will never be denied, and if that individual requests another family member, or all the other family members to come along, full cooperation will always be given.

You should assume that you have this same right, even if it has never been negotiated and agreed to in advance. But, if your parent refuses, to whom can you turn? Try talking to a grandparent, guidance counselor, school psychologist or social worker, teacher, athletic coach, scoutmaster, physician or minister, for starters. You have the right to be heard! If no one is paying attention to you at home, you should be free to seek help from an outsider who can listen and, if necessary, advocate for you.

Recurring Stepfamily Themes

I've Failed—Although children may voice approval of a parent's plan to remarry, they are rarely—if ever—prepared for the actual event and its inevitable consequences.

As I noted earlier, children generally feel at least partly responsible for a divorce. Also, they are almost always hoping for, and working toward, a reconciliation of their parents. To have to let go of that dream can be very difficult. It represents failure—a failure to get the parents back together, again.

Some kids don't let go of it, but do anything they can to drive the stepparent from the home. Others deal with the remarriage by shifting their loyalty and attention primarily to the still-unmarried other parent.

~ ~ ~

In one situation I worked with, a single father had custody of a son for 5 years before he remarried. Within 2 months of the wedding, the 13-year-old boy was having serious school problems and had announced his intention to move in with his single mother.

He thought he could get a better deal from his mother; escape his school problems and start over in a new school; punish his father for destroying his reconciliation fantasy; and take care of his mother, who obviously needed him more than his father did, since she was still all alone. (This lands him right in that man-of-the-house trap we discussed earlier.)

~ ~ ~

We know from experience that all of this can go on at the subconscious level, without any conscious awareness on the part of you kids. But, what can you do about this problem? Try to avoid having any hidden agenda for you parents; you have enough to worry about already. If you can truly accept the divorce, you won't feel that you have failed when a parent remarries.

Which Family?—As long as your parents are married and living together in the same house as their unmarried children, there is no question as to what constitutes the family. However, following a divorce and the remarriage of at least one parent, things start to get fuzzy.

When working with a stepfamily, I have occasionally asked each member to list the names of everyone in his or her family. Almost inevitably, each list is different.So, to begin with at least, a stepfamily is more a collection of unrelated people than is a traditional family. If you want to carry this on a bit, you come to the strange realization that, although your parents may now be married to new partners, they continue to relate to you pretty much as single parents.

A father realized this for the first time when he took his son to a summer family-camp. The boy's stepmother wanted to attend, but remained at home so as to be present for the birth of her first grandchild. When asked if he was a single parent, he said he was not, and explained the circumstances surrounding his wife's absence; however, he was uncomfortable with his answer because he realized he felt like a single parent. After struggling with this ambiguity, he finally cleared his head by noting to himself that he was a single parent that just happened to be married to another single parent. He was pleased to be married to his new wife, but was beginning to give up the romantic notion that their two families would ever become *one big happy family*.

He began to see this when he and his wife planned the first *family Christmas* celebration of their new life together. Now he understood and *really* accepted it. He discussed this with his wife, who also felt relieved by this novel way of looking at things. But, there was a note of sadness in having to let go of the fantasy of creating an ideal family out of a collection of people. It may work sometimes, for some people, under some circumstances—but not very often.

This is an example of the sort of thing that should be addressed during premarital counseling. To do so might head off a lot of grief. When I discuss this issue with couples, there is a significant reduction in the amount of guilt and sense of personal failure they exhibit. People need to realize that some of their expectations are simply too unrealistic. And when they are able to let go of these, they feel very relieved. Psychologists call this *reframing*, which is a fancy term for moving over and looking at a situation from a new vantage point.

What Do I Call Them?—Children who live with parents during their formative years share with them in the development of nicknames and terms of endearment which suggest a certain amount of intimacy and trust. Outsiders do not use these terms; their use is restricted. The same can be said for relatives and close friends. Each one's special name, nickname or title, tends to identify the person and to define the nature of the relationship. So what does one do with stepparents? Some do not like to be called by their first names; and Mr. or Mrs. sounds so formal. It can be a problem.

It seems logical that the answer ought to be: whatever is mutually acceptable. But, all too often a zealous new stepfather (I've never known a stepmother who did this) insists on being called *Dad*, or *Father*. I've even known a few stepfathers who forbad the stepchildren to speak openly, in front of them, of their fathers. A position like this is obviously indefensible, but some stepfathers will take it—and the new stepchildren get alienated in the process. Here again, stepparents who have been through premarital counseling will probably be more sensitive.

If you are pushed, a response might be, "Someone else already has a claim to that title; can't we come up with a different one for you?" If this does not lead to a mutually acceptable resolution, try discussing it with one or both of your natural parents. If this still does not solve it, go back and re-read the section, *Help For Yourself,* at the beginning of this chapter. Hold your ground, if necessary, and insist on an arrangement everyone is comfortable with.

"You're Not My Real Parent—so I don't have to listen to you," is a common theme in stepfamilies, and it can mean lots of things.

It is clearly a challenge, and a way of saying, "You're trying to take my father's place, and I'm not going to allow you to do that." Or, "I want to see my father and mother get back together again, so why should I make your life easier?" Or, "I'm angry at having to let go of the authority, freedom and power I had around here before you came along." Or, "Since you barged in here, you've been cutting into the time I used to have with my father; and I resent that." Or, "I'm not going to betray my mother by getting close to you."

Regardless of what it means to question the authority of a stepparent, the confrontation by the stepchild provides a good opportunity for the stepparent to listen, and thereby come to understand what is going on, which might then lead to a resolution. But, too often, anger begets an angry response, which inevitably makes matters worse.

If you get caught in this bind, wouldn't it be better to identify your underlying feeling and express *that*, rather than to mask it with an angry conversation stopper?

And when it comes to authority, it might be good to remember that one doesn't have to be a parent in order to enforce house rules that have been agreed to by both spouses, any more than a dorm parent at school has to be a biological parent of each student.

What we're talking about here seems to be more of a problem when parent and children lived in the residence before the stepparent moved in. That is always a very risky thing to do, even though there may be no other option at the time. The stepchildren view the newcomer as an outsider and intruder who disrupts established schedules and routines. The stepparent, on the other hand, feels that he or she is living in a house haunted by the ghost of a former resident. It is better by far, if at all possible, for members of a stepfamily to begin their shared life together in a residence that is new to all of them. This way, they all start off even, with fewer established patterns for the stepparent to have to adjust to.

In working with parents or stepparents, I urge them not to interfere with each other's parenting style, but to let each one be responsible for his or her own relationship to the children or stepchildren. This tends to reduce conflict, but does not mean that anyone is free to be abusive or neglectful.

The Right To Be Loved—As we said in chapter 5, you have a right to expect certain things from another person with whom you share a caring relationship. Then, in chapter 7, we identified six enforceable rights, without any mention of the previous list of expectations. Is there a conflict? No, and here's why. The last of those aforementioned six rights was *love*; but how do you define love? It is certainly very subjective—at best. That is , you know when you feel loved, and it is more than just being treated courteously. It is more than just being treated honestly. It is more than just being liked, although love certainly includes all of these. If you want to get philosophical, you could even say that love is more than the sum of its parts. It is all of that list of expectations, and much more.

Clearly, love cannot be legislated or mandated, yet we feel that everyone has a right to be loved.

Suppose you have a friendship that turns sour, where you begin to feel neglected, taken for granted and tolerated, more than cared for—what do you do? You probably back off, let that relationship cool, and begin to look elsewhere for something better. But if you're a young person who feels that way about a parent or stepparent, it's more complicated. "Do you love me?" will probably be met with a recitation of all the things he or she does for you. Sound off to someone outside the family and that person might also recite a list of all the good things that are done for you at home.To remind you of all these things doesn't help, because you know that a feeling of being loved does not come from whatever rights, privileges and gratuities you enjoy. It is more. It comes from knowing that you are valued and cherished.

So, you can feel lonely in a crowd; and you can still need a lot of loving reassurance, even in a family. Sometimes you need more than you are getting; sometimes more than your parents and/or stepparents are able to provide at the moment.

Remember the young man who had four homes-away-from-home, that I told you about earlier? I didn't mention in that story that while this young man's parents were going through their divorce, these families were his lifesavers. I hope that you have at least one such relationship. Although you have the right to be loved, sometimes you may have to reach out to find that love. But, of this you may be sure, it is always out there—if you look for it and are receptive to it when you find it.

Conflicting House Rules—When you are a part of two families, you are apt to experience reentry problems as you move back and forth. This is normal and understandable, but it seems only fair that your parents should try to keep differences to an absolute minimum in areas that affect you. This certainly includes your expectations and house rules. Ideally, they will collaborate on these things for your sake and theirs; but if they could do this they would probably still be married to each other. So, again, what do you do? As before, I would encourage openness on your part in these matters. If it is serious enough, talk to someone outside the family.

Summary

Where there are children, the dissolution of a marriage and the subsequent restructuring of the entire family is typically an incredibly painful and difficult experience. And when one or both parents remarry, everyone is usually shocked to find that adding a stepparent to the equation doesn't automatically resolve anything.

Relationships still have to be developed; communication skills are still needed. And the working assumptions one used in the former home may not work in the new one.

In this chapter, we have focused on trying to understand and make the best of this process, which admittedly is not easy to pull off.

In the opening paragraph of this chapter, I alluded to the many fine books on divorce that are available. Browse through your local library or bookstore for some of these. Talk with your school psychologist, social worker or guidance counselor about which books might be best for you, depending on your particular interest or need. But no matter how much reading you do, you will still need to work on successful relationships with your parents and stepparents.

Constructive Communication

We're communicating something all the time, even when we don't realize it, even when there are no words. But, are we aware of what we are saying? Is it what we want to say? If so, will it accomplish its purpose, or be counterproductive?

In the previous eight chapters we have tried to shed a little light on the mystery of parental behavior. This may help you to understand your parents better, and even to predict or anticipate some of the things they might do under certain circumstances in the future. We have suggested possible responses you might consider making in specific situations, as well as given support for your right to have reasonable expectations for your relationships.

Now, let's go a step further and suggest that, in order to enjoy the highest quality of interaction with others—including parents, we need to have at our disposal a repertoire of communication skills which can be used selectively to help us achieve our goals.

These skills can be learned in only two ways: from your parents, if you are lucky enough to have parents who have learned them and who use them routinely around the home, which is the exception rather than the rule; or by taking a course on the subject at school or at some other community institution. Notice, please, that I did not say you can learn these skills by reading a book. You really need a group experience where you can practice with others under the guidance of an experienced instructor. From these programs, you can expect to develop a battery of skills that will enhance your competence in human relations for the rest of your life.

Many colleges and universities offer such courses for credit or for personal enrichment. High schools, town libraries, community centers and churches also offer similar training events to the general public. The college level courses are probably developed by the instructor. In most cases, community-based courses are designed by specialists and offered through a network of trained teachers.

My own experience suggests that such a franchised program of instruction is superior to the home-made variety because it has been standardized, tested and refined over a long period of time, as the result of constant feedback from both participants and instructors.

I think it was during the summer of 1970 that I attended an intensive two-week course in marriage and family counseling offered jointly by Pepperdine University and the American Institute of Family Relations in Los Angeles. One of the presenters was psychologist Dr. Thomas Gordon, who had recently completed his now-well-known book, *Parent Effectiveness Training.* I was impressed by his model and the ambitious program he was developing and offering to parents through an expanding cadre of professional persons around the country: educators, clergy and mental health workers.

After my orientation, I began to offer Parent Effectiveness Training courses at the counseling center where I was director, and I used the P.E.T. model with couples and families who were seeing me for therapy. As an Approved Supervisor for the American Association for Marriage and Family Therapy, I often included participation in a P.E.T. course as part of the graduate and postgraduate training I offered candidates for membership; these trainees have repeatedly reported that the 8- to 10-session course was the most useful and practical of all the graduate courses they had taken. Since I did not design the course, I can make this statement without claiming credit for myself.

Dr. Gordon has gone on to adapt his model to other populations, including teachers, human beings in general, leaders, *and young people.* Different manuals, workbooks and audio-visual have been designed for each course, although the same communication model is basic to all of them.

At the time of this writing *Youth Effectiveness Training* is being revised; for information on this, or any Effectiveness Training course, write to Effectiveness Training Associates at the address given in the Appendix. Because of the cost of promoting and recruiting students for these courses, the fastest way to have one offered in your area is line up enough interested friends, and ask Effectiveness Training Associates to supply you with information and promotional literature, and the name of their nearest instructor. Or, see your school psychologist, social worker or guidance counselor, clergyperson or youth director about sponsoring a course in your community. An ideal situation would be for the sponsoring organization to schedule two courses at the same time: one for parents, and one for youth. This way, both you and your parents come out of the separate experiences speaking and understanding the same language.

The Effectiveness Training model, among other things, zeros in on four distinct abilities: listening skills, confrontation skills, conflict resolution skills and skills for dealing with a collision of values.

If you think *listening* is easy, just reflect on how difficult it is to get someone to take you seriously enough to really listen to what you say.

When it comes to *confrontation*, in this context, we're not talking about giving the other person an unsolicited piece of your mind, but something much more constructive.

Many *conflicts* are resolved (probably only temporarily) on the basis of who has the most power: one person wins and the other loses. Gordon's model calls for win-win solutions to our inevitable conflicts, so that no one goes away mad.

Values clashes do not have to signal the end of a relationship. They can be dealt with so that opposing viewpoints will be accepted, and, where possible, respected. In some cases, of course, relationships are suspended, or sometimes ended when a collision of values is over an issue of really major proportions. But at least, with Gordon's model, the chance of this happening is greatly reduced.

Note: I stand to gain absolutely nothing by plugging Tom Gordon's Effectiveness Training enterprise. I do it solely because of the great respect I have for it, which in turn arises out of the many success stories I have witnessed in the lives of individuals who have made a serious attempt to use his model in their lives.

Loose Ends

This chapter might also be called Et Cetera, Odds and Ends, Smorgasbord or Potpourri. It's about issues that do not warrant an entire chapter, yet should not be completely overlooked. The first of these has to do with ...

Reinventing the Wheel

I was in the company of a friend as we walked past a romantically inclined couple oblivious to our presence. He grunted and said, "Today's kids seem to think they discovered sex!" I guess that's one thing everyone has to discover, but a lot of things once discovered are here to stay and do not need to be reinvented—like the wheel. An adaptation of this says, "He who ignores history is doomed to repeat it." In a sense, the history of civilization is the record of building upon the discoveries of previous generations and trying to learn from their successes and failures. However, sometimes it doesn't work as it should. For example, why do we have to rediscover peace? How many wars will it take before the inhabitants of this planet really learn to get along together?

Coyote, of *Roadrunner* cartoon fame, has the same problem; he has no sense of history. He tries again and again to outwit his prey, but every effort ends with the situation (sometimes literally) blowing up in his face. Maybe this is why he is so popular—he is so much like the rest of us.

I am especially concerned when I see a young person playing Coyote by engaging in what is obviously a high-risk activity, or a self-defeating and self-destructive behavior. Yes, I understand intellectually why a person might behave this way, but it still makes me sad when I see someone who appears to be bent on learning *everything* the hard way—unable or unwilling to profit from the experience of others, including parents. Eventually, the lesson may be learned, but it is frequently at great cost and after much pain.

Perhaps you would be more interested in learning how we parents resolve our own ethical and moral dilemmas if we could resist the temptation to tell you how to handle yours. I'm convinced that young people can come up with pretty creative decisions, as long as they have sufficient information upon which to base them. Too often, parents give answers without taking the time to help their kids develop the skills and acquire the knowledge to think things through for themselves.

So, here again, unfortunately, the burden falls back upon you. I urge you to voice your concerns and at least try to discuss them with your parents and other adults. Also, show an interest in their stories, and learn all you can from their experiences. It could clear up some confusion that you have; and when adults start to preach and give you unsolicited advice, just try to let them know honestly how it feels. That's better than tuning them out.

As we discussed earlier, it is easy to defy parents and behave in passive aggressive ways when we're angry. So, I want to remind you again to slow down and *think* before you rush out and behave recklessly—especially when it is something that others before you have tried, only to get mauled. You really need an enlightened self-interest in order to keep yourself on track. If you can maintain that, maybe you won't need to waste time reinventing the wheel.

Keep Your Battery Charged

Four years ago I purchased a computer that I am just now starting to use. Many frustrating and totally unproductive hours were spent trying to figure out why I was too stupid to make it work as it should. I could not even handle a word processing program that my son's fifth grade teacher had recommended *for him*. After several conversations with the gentleman who had sold me the equipment, I sat down at my computer, telephone in hand, and followed—step by step—his instructions.

Rather quickly he exclaimed, "Oh, I see your problem, your battery is run down! When that happens, the computer forgets who it is, and does all kinds of crazy things."

It's possible for the same thing to happen to us. We let our batteries get run down to the point where we can't remember who we are. Then crazy, erratic or inappropriate behavior results. If we are to live fulfilling and productive lives, we *must* keep our batteries charged. We must remember who we are.

How? First of all there is the obvious: proper nutrition and balanced meals, exercise, adequate sleep, good human relations. But there is more, for we have been told that humankind does not live by bread alone. This refers, of course, to our spiritual dimension—a part of us which can only be neglected at great risk.

There are many ways to nurture one's spirit: inspirational reading, meditation, listening to great music, gardening, playing an instrument, attendance at the theater, participation in religious services or rituals, stimulating conversation with a friend, involvement in some community service activity, a visit to an art exhibit, development of some creative interest or hobby—or just a relaxing walk in the out-of-doors.

That last one is increasingly important for those of us who live in cities, as it is too easy to lose our connectedness to the web of life, which inevitably leaves us feeling isolated and fragmented. So whether it is a walk by the seashore, silently watching a sunset, or visiting some famous botanical garden or national park, we need at least an occasional experience of reconnecting with that which is basic and timeless.

For example, I will never forget my train ride through the Canadian Rockies from Calgary to Banff. The late afternoon trip took less than an hour, but as we drew closer to our destination the distant purple mountains were transformed from a subdued rugged outline on the horizon into towering majestic walls of almost perpendicular rock which completely blocked the direct rays of the sun. That experience was so moving and unnerving as to be almost spooky.

I think the internationally acclaimed photographer, Galen Rowell, was referring to what I experienced when he recently wrote:

> Ordered natural forms strike universal cords within us that the photographic critic Robert Adams identifies as answers to "our worst fear," the suspicion that life may be chaos, and that therefore our suffering is without meaning.

So, however you do it, please take the time to keep your battery charged. If you let it run down, you may find, like the computer, that you have a tough time remembering who you really are. And that is no way to live.

The Empty Nest

This is a reality that is always coming. But, like death, few think about it or prepare for it. I guess folks figure it is something that will happen, all in good time. And, of course, it usually does.

I have never seen statistics on the subject, but I suspect that an increasingly large number of young people continue to live with their parents after completing high school, whether they go on to college or not. The rationale given for this is simply that it is cheaper.

While it clearly costs less to live at home, few young people have the self-discipline to stash away the cash they are saving by staying with their parents. I have known many cases where that extra money was invested in the down payment on an expensive car, followed by a monthly financial commitment so high that the individual could not afford to move out, or to contribute to the cost of his or her maintenance. Almost inevitably this led to frayed nerves and conflict.

Sometimes, such an arrangement continues until the young person decides to marry. This can be very risky, at best, because then he or she has not experienced the reality of being on one's own, where money must be stretched, choices made, priorities established and discipline exercised. In the case of a daughter, she may enter into marriage expecting to be taken care of as she was at home; for a son, he may expect his wife to do likewise. Neither of them may be ready for the abrupt and unavoidable changes coming their way.

Both young men and young women need a time interval between leaving home and getting married that gives them a chance to develop the experience and survival skills necessary to succeed in the real world. Trying to learn these things *after* marriage puts too great a strain on the relationship.

This is not something you have to do on your own; you can find one or two others to share the cost with you. My two oldest children—daughters, born one year apart—took this route, after finding a third young woman to join with them in their new adventure. An adventure it was! And for me it was a real eye-opener. As these three young women struggled to develop a working relationship, my daughters discussed their experiences with me individually. What I heard was the identical litany of complaints that I listen to in my office from married couples. This helped me to understand that human dynamics are pretty much the same, whether two people are of the opposite sex or same sex, married or unmarried, sexually active or not.

So, while this book is not intended to be a premarital guidebook, it is safe to say that one cannot help but be better prepared for marriage if he or she is better prepared for life in general.

While my wife and I were having breakfast recently, we heard a terrible ruckus break out in our large backyard. It sounded like a bunch of crows fighting with each other. Investigation revealed that it was a family of crows: two adults and about five smaller ones—not babies by a long shot, but not adults either. They were all on the ground, with the adults trying their level best to teach their youngsters how to forage for food. The young ones were screeching at the top of their lungs, obviously wanting to be fed; but the parents stood their ground, patiently showing them how it was to be done. Eventually the kids got the word and gave it a try: reluctantly and angrily to be sure, but they did it. As they gave in, one by one, the noise subsided, with the whole show lasting about 40 minutes.

Since your emancipation is coming one way or another, why fight it like the young crows did? Plan for it, so that you can do it on your terms. And you know what? If you do, your parents may be so supportive of the decision that they will give you a hand with the initial expenses of setting up housekeeping—they can be considerable!

The Devil Made Me Do It

In a recent cartoon Andy Capp returned home later than expected and obviously under the influence. As usual, he had to face an angry wife, to whom he gave this excuse: "It wasn't *my* fault, Pet. I ran into this old army pal and he insisted we have one, then another, then another."

Flo interrupted with, "All right, all right, get ta' bed." Then she mumbled to herself, "Nothing causes more trouble around here than the other bloke."

For most of us, there's too much of a tendency to blame someone else for what *we* do. Thus, "the devil made me do it," or "Joe talked me into it." Some of us will do anything to avoid responsibility for our own actions.

This is another version of the same mentality that I hear expressed with great regularity. Only yesterday a mother in her seventies said to me, "I guess I spoiled my daughter when she was a child, but I couldn't help myself; that's the way I am."

Recently, a husband excused the beating he gave his wife by stating, "I didn't know what I was doing; I was drunk."

In working with families, I have found that there is something very malignant about blame. It seems to work this way:

1. Once you begin to blame another person for your own unhappiness, the focus of your attention is on what is wrong with him or her (or human nature or society in general) rather than on trying to resolve the problem.
2. The more you repeat the accusation, the more you tend to believe it.
3. The more you blame, the more you find to blame.
4. Blaming often leads to anger and vindictiveness.
5. This leads to a sense of paralysis, helplessness, and eventually, to hopelessness; for a solution is now seen as being in the hands of another, who can't or won't change.

My own rule of thumb on this subject is that unless someone uses force, trickery or deceit to take advantage of me, I'd better not waste time blaming. Feeling disappointed—yes; blaming—a waste of time! It's better to focus on what I can do about it, and where I can go with it from here. I may not be completely to blame for the mess I'm in, but getting out of that mess is *my* responsibility, and mine alone. Others may help, but they can't do it for me.

Therefore, watch out for blaming; it's a dead-end street.

Abuse and Neglect

It is Edmund Burke who is credited with having first said, "The only thing necessary for evil to triumph in the world is for good people to do nothing." What that means in terms of abuse is that unless a bully is stopped, he can only be expected to keep on bullying.

So how do you deal with a bully? You basically already know how—just reflect back on your school experiences. When a bigger kid wouldn't stop bullying one of my sons, he assembled a few of his friends and together they served notice that a subsequent attack on any one of them would be answered with a very decisive collective response. It worked, and the bully left them alone. In a sense, this is what society tries to do on a larger scale: it is organized in such a way as to provide collective security and to protect individual rights. But some people don't know how to connect with the system; others are afraid to trust it, as in the following cases.

~ ~ ~

> A woman, at 16 years of age, grew tired of witnessing her father's abusive behavior toward her mother. She was afraid to ask for family, police or community help, and took matters into her own hands by telling her father that if he did it again she would kill him. Not deterred by his angry daughter's threat, the father did attack the mother one last time, about a week later. His daughter literally blew off his head with one blast from his shotgun. Although she was found by the court to have acted in self-defense, she has spent the remainder of her life wishing she had tried another approach first.

She might have gone to someone else in the family or neighborhood, or even her minister, since hers was a rather religious community. But she didn't, and now she must live with that tragic decision.

~ ~ ~

A Baptist minister in Florida was approached by a female member of his parish with a tale of an abusive husband and fresh bruises to back up her story. The minister tried to comfort the woman, and promised that he would have a talk with her wayward husband, assuring her that it would *never* happen again.

In the company of three God-fearing deacons, he made a pastoral visit to the home, where he read some passages from the Bible, prayed for the man, and exhorted him to renounce his sinful ways and henceforth live a godly life appropriate for a Christian husband. Then the four of them prepared to depart, with the minister leaving first. The other three lingered only long enough for one of them to say, "And brother Charles: just one more thing. If we have to return, you can count on this for sure—we'll break both your legs!"

~ ~ ~

Although what these four men did was very illegal, I'm told that it worked; for this is the kind of approach that bullies understand. They came to be the people they are because along the way parents and others made excuses for them and failed to hold them accountable for their behavior. If a credible threat is made against them, most will get the message and back off. In the former case, the father didn't believe his daughter and lost his life. In the latter one, the abusive husband believed the deacons and didn't try it again.

While on the surface this church story may seem to some to be the worst kind of vigilante behavior, it is precisely the method used by society in general for dealing with abusive persons. The only difference is that the programs used by court, probation and social service personnel are legal, more sophisticated, more time consuming, and more expensive. But the bottom-line message of many, if not most, so-called rehabilitation programs, is the same as that given by the burly deacons: Don't even *think* about doing it again—or else!

But remember, if we take the law into our own hands, we are apt to end up on the wrong side of the criminal justice system. If the criminal justice system does it, it has due process and the law on its side.

America has been experiencing such a breakdown of law and order in some cities that beleaguered, fed-up citizens are organizing themselves into groups dedicated to cleaning up their own neighborhoods; and it is working! Of course this works best when such groups work within the law and cooperate with the police—for due process must be respected if we are to avoid a complete return to the jungle.

Therefore, if you are involved in, or are aware of, an abusive situation, at least give society a chance by reporting the incident to a responsible person such as a school guidance counselor, psychologist or social worker. And don't take the law into your own hands except in an emergency situation. Even then, be very, very careful; the law expects you to use force to protect yourself or another person *only* when there is no other alternative. Furthermore, you are expected to use *no more force than is necessary* to bring the situation under control. Anything more than this could get you into serious trouble. So, please remember:

1. Abuse is illegal.
2. Abuse can be stopped.
3. No one should tolerate abuse.
4. Help is available to everyone—victim or abuser.
5. Suffering in silence is the worst of all possible responses to abuse.
6. Share this message with anyone who needs to hear it.

Some One-Liners

I'd like to conclude this chapter, and Part One, with these quick thoughts. They come from a variety of sources, and most of them have been around from quite some time; I think they capture, in just a few words, the essence of some of the things I've tried to say here. They are fairly easy to recall, and are quite to the point. Some have appeared in earlier chapters, and I repeat them here for you convenience.

> "A family is not a democracy."
>
> ***William Freebairn***

> "Life is like a bicycle. You don't fall off unless you stop peddling."
>
> ***Claude Pepper***

> "Unhappiness is the ultimate form of self-indulgence."
>
> ***Tom Robbins***

> "When nobody around you seems to measure up, it's time to check your yardstick."
>
> ***Bill Lemley***

> "No problem is so big or complicated that it can't be run away from."
>
> ***Linus (Peanuts)***

> "We either grow, or we die."
>
> ***Henry Miller***

> "The rung of the ladder was never meant to rest upon, but only to hold a person's foot long enough to enable him to put the other somewhat higher."
>
> ***Thomas Huxley***

> "Maturity is the ability to live in someone else's world."
>
> ***Oren Arnold***

> "Ninety-nine percent of the failures come from people who have the habit of making excuses."
>
> ***George Washington Carver***

"Take good care of your future because that is where you're going to spend the rest of your life."

C. F. Kettering

"The only thing necessary for evil to triumph in the world is for good people to do nothing."

Edmund Burke

"Unless you are prepared to accept no for an answer, your request is only a disguised order."

Thomas Gordon

"Love is a game that two can play and both win."

Eva Gabor

"Learn good things; the bad will teach you by themselves."

An old Russian proverb

PART TWO

Primarily for Parents

About Part Two

Although Part One was addressed to young people, all of it represented appropriate reading for parents. On the other hand, there are some thoughts I should like to share with parents that would have been out of place in the previous chapters.

Additionally, questions may have been raised in the minds of parents by the earlier material, that can be dealt with here.

This does not mean that Part Two is an adults-only section. On the contrary, there are no secrets here. And as I have learned from my practice, having only partial knowledge of what is going on can cause one to imagine the worst. So it can do no harm for kids to know what I am saying to their parents. In fact, I encourage it.

Observations and suggestions in this section are in many cases applicable to children of any age. The principles are the same; only the application differs.

Prior to publication, I asked a number of parents to read Part One, and to give me feedback on the kinds of concerns and unanswered questions they had after reading it. Without exception, these issues are dealt with in the following chapters.

Punishment Reconsidered

In the chapter called, *Rights, Duties, Privileges, Gratuities,* I focused on the interplay between compliance with family rules and the enjoyment of privileges. In discussing withdrawal of a privilege, I admitted that this is technically punishment, but that I prefer to think of it as suspension of privileges. This notion is more palatable to me because I can't understand how one inflicts punishment on someone by suspending a privilege that was—by its very definition—optional and gratuitous to begin with. It is not the parents' fault if their child confuses his rights with his privileges.

I know the pained expression a kid can wear as he or she attempts to push a parental guilt button with something like, "You really know how to hurt me, don't you!" Such a statement is a real hooker, because the word *hurt* grabs you where you are most vulnerable; in your earliest training you were taught not to hurt others. The solution? Unless you've really lost it and physically struck your child, don't buy into that *hurt* routine. Insist instead that the word *disappoint* be used, for your child may indeed be disappointed with your position! Try this. You will find it easier to live with unpopular decisions.

Here are some more distinctions right out of the dictionary that you might find useful:

Punish implies the infliction of some penalty on a wrongdoer and generally connotes retribution rather than correction;

Discipline suggests punishment that is intended to control or to establish habits of self-control;

Correct suggests punishment for the purpose of overcoming faults;

Chastise usually implies corporal punishment and connotes both retribution and correction;

Castigate now implies punishment by severe public criticism or censure;

Chasten implies the infliction of tribulation in order to make another obedient, meek, etc.

You do with these distinctions as you wish. As for me, I prefer to keep external control to an absolute minimum, and to maximize internal control and decision-making powers. The judicious handling of privileges can be quite effective in shaping self-discipline, and can go a long way toward eliminating fear in the parent-child relationship. Children will, for the most part, allow parents a great deal of latitude in the things they say and do. So personally, if I'm going to err, I'd rather do it in the direction of too little control than to find out later that I have been too harsh and punitive.

I realize that some may disagree with me on this subject, and I'm not going to be mad about that. But to those who want to stay with punishment as a legitimate routine approach to shaping behavior in children, I offer the following thoughts. If you feel that you have to punish unacceptable behavior:

1. Then also reward acceptable behavior! Otherwise punishment could become the primary form of attention the child receives. This could definitely warp the child emotionally, resulting in his or her having to misbehave in order to receive attention. Animal trainers know this. And to limit one's parental responses to punishment for undesirable behavior will only confuse children, make them afraid, and definitely fail to let them know what behavior *is* expected.

2. Make sure the child knows the reason for the punishment, otherwise the message that gets conveyed is that you disapprove of *him* or *her*.
3. Never punish in anger! If you do, the punishment will probably be too severe, resulting in resentment in the child and further acting out as a form of protest, or as an attempt to get back at you. But if you should fail at this point and later feel that you have been unfair, don't be afraid to say so and to apologize if necessary. You are human. Don't be afraid to admit it to your child.
4. Get the whole story, lest you punish the wrong person or punish inappropriately.
5. As discussed earlier, try to do so by withdrawing a privilege. This way, the child has an incentive to change the problem behavior in order to earn back the suspended privilege.
6. Remember that violence begets violence. Do you want your child to use violence on his siblings and friends as a way of resolving conflict?
7. Hear the child out. At least accept and respect his/her feelings. Don't expect him or her to like being punished. If negative feelings cannot be expressed verbally, they will surely be expressed later in oblique forms of behavior which will only prolong, confuse and escalate the conflict.
8. You are locking your child into a system of behavior based on what someone else thinks is best. As such ...
    a. Who will take over your role in the child's life if you die or the child leaves home?
    b. Can you be sure a surrogate will truly love your child, and not exploit her for selfish, possibly destructive, ends?

c. At what point will the child be ready to exercise his own independent judgment as to what is best for him, if he has always been able to depend upon you for that information?

d. What happens when the grandchildren are born, and your grandchildren's children?

Question: When will she ever grow up?

Possible Answer: Has she really ever had a chance?

Simply put, punishment is pretty risky at best, and can be very destructive. It never really works, if the object of parenting is to raise self-reliant, self-confident and healthy children, and punishment is always perceived by the child as bullying.

There is a better way. And it is not to be found in going to the other extreme and raising children permissively by letting *them* be bullies and tyrants.

Somewhere in between these two extremes children can be treated as people: with dignity, patience, love and respect. They will respond, because kids are beautiful; but like all living things, they respond best to tender loving care.

This approach to parenting rarely comes easily. It takes commitment and hard work. It may take involvement in some kind of professionally led, structured learning experience, where the necessary communication skills can be mastered.

This takes time and costs a little money. Are children worth it? Some parents don't seem to think so, and this is a tragedy. Too many people will spend thousands of dollars on remedial treatment after their commonsense parenting methods fail, but so few are willing to take a little bit of time and spend a small amount of money *now* to develop the skills that can help lay a foundation for healthy children, contented parents, and happy homes.

If Not You, Who? If Not Now, When?

Occasionally I encounter a serious problem with parents who are afraid their children are not yet ready for the structure I recommend. Having been relatively unstructured parents in the past, they are now reluctant to go to the other extreme too suddenly.

When I suggest bringing the children to the next session, I may hear something like, "They have already served notice that they want nothing to do with this. So there is no way we can make them come." I don't question this, but respond with, "That may well be, but you can sure make them wish they had come!" How? By starting to yank privileges right now!

You don't need to make a big deal of it by threatening or announcing your determination in advance. You just wait—and quietly say *no* next time a youngster asks for a favor. Explain the connection, if necessary, and if you get a promising, whining and pleading reaction, just say, "What is it about *no* that you don't understand?" He or she will get the message.

~ ~ ~

A mother and stepfather had just completed the paperwork for an expensive 30-day Outward Bound experience for their 16-year-old son, Fred. They had read success stories from the organization and were desperate for anything that offered some hope. Fred had also reviewed the literature and was asked to sign a consent form, at which point he started to drag his feet. I suspect that he wanted to make some kind of deal, like maybe throwing a big going-away bash for his friends; but the parents simply took the papers and said nothing. In less than 10 minutes the boy said to his stepfather, "How about giving me a ride

> to Denny's?" His stepfather responded with, "Why should I do that for you when you won't cooperate with us?" The boy then replied, "Give me the paper; I'll sign it." He got his ride. He also went through Outward Bound.
>
> The parents of this lad also wanted him to accompany them to see their family therapist. After his initial refusal, they again held back on an important privilege. When he protested, Mother said, "You could always go with us to see Dr. Zook, and tell him yourself what miserable parents you have." Without any hesitation he replied, "I'll do it!"

~ ~ ~

So, if you get resistance, there are ways to obtain cooperation in your effort to establish a structure for your family. You do not have to wait until everything is in place and clearly understood.

Another concern some parents have is whether or not children will react negatively to what may be perceived as a sudden crackdown. In its most severe form, one or both parents may fear that a child may become defiant, destructive, a runaway or even suicidal. Or there may be a fear that such a structure is something a particular child simply may not be able to handle.

One response to this parental dilemma is for me to reassure parents that other alternatives open to the child aren't any better; in fact, they are usually much worse. Life on the streets is no picnic. Life in a foster home or institution of any kind is far more structured than anything I have suggested. So, as long as there is no abuse or neglect, and as long as there is no suicide threat, there isn't a great deal to worry about.

What about suicide? My rule of thumb is that a threat or gesture should never be ignored or taken lightly. As I explained in Part One: to fail to take suicide talk seriously may cause the child to feel trapped, and obliged to up the ante with a reckless overt act of some kind that could result in miscalculated serious harm, or even death.

You might—therefore—report it to a family physician or therapist, either of whom should be familiar enough with your community resources to give you some direction and guidance. You definitely should not try to handle this one alone. So much for a kid's attempt to blackmail parents with suicide threats.

Something I have occasionally done in response to other forms of resistance in kids, is to schedule a conference with a probation officer from juvenile court. The parents, the child and I go to the courthouse, where a sympathetic, yet stern officer of the court spells out in graphic detail what happens when parents ask for help with a *stubborn child.* Without exception, this powerful experience has had a profoundly positive effect upon the child. In every case, it completely neutralized any lingering doubt in the child's mind as to how this game is played. Court personnel have been most cooperative. They too would rather engage in preventive intervention with children. This is something that may be possible in your state. If you have exhausted all your other options, you might want to look into it—especially if you are a single parent.

Of all the institutions with which I am familiar (including the military, mental hospitals, foster homes, prisons, boarding schools) there is not one where privileges do not have to be earned! What other *way* is there to learn what responsibility and accountability are all about? What better *place* is there to learn it than in the home, where there is hopefully a foundation of love and compassion to undergird the structure and make it more humane? If not you, who? If not now, when?

Selected Commentary on Part One

Expectations

In the chapter called, *If You Love Me You Will,* we discussed a list of expectations in detail. That material is basic to the structure I have recommended, so I hope you have read it carefully and digested it.

If you are married and living with your spouse, I should think that it is rather important for the two of you to have reached an agreement of some kind as to what you expect of one another. It is important as the basis for a smooth-functioning marriage; and it is equally important in terms of the example it sets for the entire family.

If you have been together long enough to have a teenager, and are still married to your child's other parent, you have probably worked this out—if not in writing, at least in principle. But if you are a single parent, you can still design your list of expectations and use it with your children. I think you will find the process of considerable value in clarifying your own thinking on the subject.

It is not uncommon for me to talk with couples who have never had a serious discussion on what they expect from one another. Each has his and her own assumptions, but they are rarely comprehensive and clear to the other person. So, if you are determined to implement this system in your family, here is the place to start—with your expectations (either joint or individual, as the case may be).

This is really about values. As such, your list may wind up being more personal than the one I presented. Just be careful that yours does not become too personalized or exclusive, lest it be seen as heavy-handed. Try for the things most of us share and would be glad to subscribe to.

Rules

Rules that are too restrictive or arbitrary can be a pain. Those that are reasonable help prevent chaos, reduce frustration, and make life run a lot smoother for everyone. So let them be realistic. Also, if there are going to be rules in your family, let them be rules and not guidelines. (Remember: Moses gave his people Ten Commandments, not Ten Suggestions.) In other words, your rules will not amount to anything more than suggestions if there is not an *or else* tied in with them. Your *or else,* of course, is the large range of options you have in terms of suspending or withholding one or more privileges.

There is really no further need for pleading with or threatening your kids, for they will know the risks if they ignore, break or forget one of the rules. Does this mean you should be mechanical and unfeeling in enforcing them? No, there is lots of room for compassion and personal judgment; but if we're not going to be serious about our rules, we would be better off without them.

For instance, in *Rights, Duties, Privileges, Gratuities,* I suggested using a sign-out board for the entire family. You may not need this, especially if your family is small. So please don't feel a need to keep a rule in your list that is unnecessary for your family. And, by all means, don't overlook one you need just because I didn't include it in my model list. Individual family variables and realities will determine the final composition of your list.

Experience may also force you to rethink certain things. Needs change as people change. Suppose, for example, a parent should move in with you. If you think that won't throw your family life for a loop, you've got some surprises coming your way. Everything is suddenly up for grabs, and the configuration in which the dust settles is definitely not the same as before the guest arrived. So flexibility is probably the order of the day.

What is the basis for all of this? In addition to the fact that your children are minors for whom you have some kind of responsibility, it wouldn't hurt to remember whose names are on the deed to your house. Theirs? Probably not. But some kids talk as though that might be the case—as did the 15-year-old girl I mentioned earlier who went to an attorney to see how she could go about having her new stepfather evicted from her home.

Now let's move on to a related subject that has to do with one of the specific rules on the model list. This one deserves special attention.

The Messy Room

What parent has not climbed the walls and swung from the chandeliers on this one! There are workable answers, and you deserve to know what they are.

I have never seen statistics on the percentage of teenagers who have private bedrooms, but I suspect the figure would be directly proportional to the family income, and inversely proportional to the number of children in the family. But whether or not children share a bedroom, the problem of the messy room continues to be a hot issue. For sure, I have never heard a parent complain that a bedroom was too neat, so I guess we could identify the basic problem as a conflict between the values of parent and child, but further complicated by an adolescent territorial imperative, a desire for privacy and a zeal for independence.

I have never seen a child react to parental complaints about the bedroom with anything other than, "Well it's my room, isn't it? I ought to be able to do what I want to with my own space!" And what parent can really argue with that? It does make sense. So I suggest yielding on any basic claim to parental jurisdiction over bedrooms, with the clear understanding that all shared space (including bathrooms) is to "be kept shipshape at all times, with the user restoring it to its normal state following use." (Rule #7 in the list of model house rules in *Rights, Duties, Privileges, Gratuities*)

But I went on to suggest that clutter "is not meant to include anything that is unsafe, potentially destructive of property, or unsanitary." These are three handles you can get on a messy room, because each has a tangible and concrete effect upon you, the parent. Unattended lit candles, overloaded electrical circuits and a skateboard on the floor are unsafe. A pile of soiled and damp clothing on the floor is potentially destructive of property. Dirty glasses, dishes and utensils are obviously unsanitary, and could easily attract bugs. You have as much right to be concerned about these things as any landlord; and that is what you are, whether your children like it or not!

After children have learned to launder, press and mend their own clothing, they seem to use hangers more frequently—but you certainly have a right (and perhaps a duty) to protect your washer and dryer from the abuse and expense of running both for only one pair of socks: something not at all unheard of.

Some parents have tried to shame kids into better habits by sharing photos of messy rooms with friends and relatives. Others have invited guests to "come upstairs and see how the rest of the family lives."

But whatever happens, and regardless of the condition of the room, you can be sure that when the children get out on their own, things usually mysteriously change for the better.

So, somewhere along the line, some kind of message gets through.

While on the subject of bedrooms, we might also consider the need for privacy. I have never known a parent who supports the idea of locks on bedroom doors, but I have heard no objections raised to the use of inside button locks which can easily be opened from the outside if necessary. Whether you go along with this or not is up to you; there are pros and cons. One thing you might consider doing is providing locked storage space for each of your children, where they can safely keep certain possessions out of the reach of predatory siblings. I know a psychiatrist who built a row of six floor-to-ceiling storage lockers in the basement for his children—each with a combination lock. For that family it worked quite well.

None of the above suggestions works equally well in all settings, even when problems are comparable. There are many variables from one family to another that will determine what, if anything, you do. My purpose here has only been to identify some things that have worked rather well for others, leaving it to you to adapt these ideas to your own needs as you see fit.

Money

It's been said that money isn't everything; but this statement is usually made by some well-to-do person who is still unhappy in spite of his wealth. I'm more inclined to appreciate the alternate version of that observation, "Money may not be everything, but it's way ahead of whatever's in second place."

Money represents power; and as such, it is really neutral. It can become a means to either good *or* evil ends, depending on one's character, how much of it one has, how it was acquired and how it is used. And if money can corrupt, so can poverty, along with a lot of other things.

Children start developing their attitudes toward money long before the teen years: but that doesn't mean it's all over as far as their monetary values are concerned. Now is the time for testing, refining and modifying those values where necessary. Parents are an essential part of that process, and have a very important contribution to make. So, let's talk specifically about money in the lives of our teenagers.

Allowances—Rule #4 (House Rules) states: *Children will be provided with a personal allowance, the amount and scope of which will be negotiated.* This leaves a lot to be negotiated, doesn't it?

In terms of *scope,* a child's first allowance is usually for personal spending money, which provides some rough idea of what things cost. It should also offer valuable lessons in the need for restraint, lest all be spent at once, leaving nothing for later in the week. As time passes, an allowance can encompass other items, such as school supplies and lunch money, haircuts, cosmetics, entertainment. There will probably be a bank account, with a requirement for saving some portion of money that is received as a gift, or as compensation for work. And before you realize it, the child's twelfth birthday has rolled around.

Even after your child has started to earn money, there are probably some things you will want to continue to fund, lest the incentive to work be lost. You might want, for example, to provide a basic clothing allowance, permitting earned income to be used to supplement your subsidy. This is a better vehicle for teaching the value of money than, say, charging a room-and-board fee before the youngster completes school, which often results in comments like, "I'm paying room and board. I ought to be able to stay in the shower as long as I want." Or, "I'm helping to buy this food; I don't know why I can't share it with my friends."

So much for scope. The amount of one's allowance obviously will depend upon the child's age, what you can afford, what it is supposed to cover, what the going rate is in your community and the cost of living where you reside. However, regardless of the scope and amount of an allowance, it should not be confused with ...

Compensation—This can come to a child from a number of sources:

1. From you—for seasonal or nonroutine tasks;
2. From a brother or sister who wants to get out of doing something, and who would rather pay for it than engage in a trade-off of services;
3. From others outside the family—for services rendered;
4. From the sale of personal property that the child has outgrown;
5. From the sale of property authorized by a parent, such as bottles.

If a parent confiscates all of a child's earnings, even for a worthy cause, where is the incentive to work? There must be some measure of short-term payoff. But after a prescribed limit, which can be negotiated, it would certainly seem reasonable for any parent to expect that a portion of compensation received be put aside for future needs (such as driver training, license and auto insurance, for example).

Most children will come to understand the real value of money only after they have had to work for it. Then they will be able to translate hours worked into such things as gallons of gasoline, jewelry, an evening on the town, a new pair of sneakers or a day at the beach.

Material Rewards—This can include financial incentives and recognition; some have even called it bribery. But whatever you call it, there is always the nagging question of whether it is acceptable, ethical and moral. Or, expressed another way, does it cause a young person to put a price tag on everything, so that he works only for the prize?

It doesn't prove anything one way or another to say so, but isn't that the way our economic and educational systems already operate? Maybe so, someone might respond, but does that mean we have to bring it into the home?

Well, even as I write I have some real reservations on the subject. For example—every time I drive by our local high school and look at the parking lot, I wonder if there are any kids left who ride the bus to school. Our children seem increasingly to have *so* much that I sometimes wonder what there is left to give them.

But, good, bad, right, wrong—who knows; it does work, and for a lot of parents, and that makes it okay. I would point out, however, that there are many nonmaterial ways to affirm, encourage, support and recognize initiative and achievement. If we were to neglect these in favor of the exclusive use of tangible monetary rewards, I think we would definitely be in *deep doodoo;* but used modestly, with discretion, and in moderation, material rewards can be effective.

Here are some situations where an award, monetary or otherwise, might be appropriate:

1. Academic achievement, however defined. Some parents establish a sliding scale for the recognition of A's and B's on report cards and/or papers and projects.
2. The successful completion of some project or course of instruction that is more important to a parent than to the child, where the award might have been negotiated in advance as an incentive. Here the child might be seen as doing onerous work for a parent, who hopes his or her youngster may come to like it.

Before we leave the subject of material rewards, I should mention that many therapeutic institutions and communities operate on the basis of what is commonly called a *token economy,* where residents are *paid* to perform desired tasks. It has been found that the *pay* does not become an end in itself. Once the desired behavior is established, it can usually be maintained by more benign and less frequent reinforcement. So, there shouldn't a great deal to worry about starting something that could get out of control.

~ ~ ~

> My youngest son had taken piano lessons for two years, and had done rather well. I had shown regular interest in his efforts, and supported them appreciatively. Then he began to make noises about wanting to quit. When I realized that he was serious and not just sounding off, we talked about it. He didn't really hate it, he'd just lost some enthusiasm, and had other interests to pursue—like Nintendo.
>
> After it seemed like he had been completely heard out, I responded. I explained that when I was his age I had complained so much about the music lessons I'd taken for 6 years that my mother finally let me quit. I told him of my regrets, and how I wish now that I had stayed with it. I explained that his sisters had gone through a similar stage in their piano lessons, but that they continued working at it until that point was reached where it started to become enjoyable instead of a chore. I explained that it was important to me that he continue—so much so that I was willing to pay him to do it, like I paid him to do lawn work.
>
> He wanted to consider it, and after a few minutes came back with a response for which I was unprepared. He said, "I don't think it's right that you should have to pay me to take piano lessons. If it's really important to you, I'll stay with it for now."
>
> Needless to say, I was pleased, and told him so. That was the first and only time I ever offered such a deal to one of my kids.

~ ~ ~

On the subject of money management, as in all values-related issues that I can think of, the example we parents set for our children is at least as important as any words we speak. If we remember this, and are clear as to where we stand on the important issues of life, we will be less likely to experience disappointment in the way our kids turn out. There are no guarantees, of course, and things frequently happen over which we have no control, but it does seem useful to try to be as consistent and congruent as possible.

Chores and Other Negotiable Issues

Rule #5 (House Rules) states: *All members of the family are expected to share in the chores necessary to maintain the household. Each one's individual responsibilities will be a matter for us to negotiate, but no one will be expected to have a disproportionate share of unpleasant tasks.*

There are several assumptions underlying this proposed rule:

1. Everyone stands to benefit from family membership; it is only fair that everyone share in the work required to maintain the unit.
2. While there are some chores that only adults can handle, there ought to be something for everyone in any division of labor.
3. Tasks should not be assigned by parents.
4. Tasks should not be assumed to be sex related. That is, who says males should not be expected to clean bathrooms and that females can't wash cars?
5. No one should be stuck permanently with an unpleasant task.
6. Children will not be paid by parents for chores.

7. Once the responsibility for a chore is accepted, it is that person's duty to either do it or have it done; having it done can mean trading off with another family member or paying another person to do it. No excuses, except in an emergency.

This may sound complicated, but when there is more than one child in the family, it can be a lot simpler than having no plan at all. However, if you don't need it, just skip it; there's no reason to over-organize.

I propose you go about implementing this—should you decide to do so—as follows:

1. With your spouse/partner (if you have one), draw up as comprehensive a list as you possibly can of *every* task that it takes to keep your family going. Include all the things done by parents that the kids won't even think of (balancing the checkbook and bank statements, for example). Include frequency of each chore. For the really big ones, like meal preparation, you might want to identify the chore as, *coordinate meal preparation*, so that others can be lined up to help with all or part of a given meal, depending on age.
2. Prepare a chart, chores across the top, and names of family members down the left side. Identify the tasks that adults need to be responsible for. Divide them up and check them off.
3. Call a meeting of the whole family. Explain what you're doing and answer questions. Be sure to explain that the distribution of chores will be for only one month. Draw straws or roll dice to see who goes first, second, etc. Then have each, in turn, choose a chore until only those tasks are left that no one wants. Write each remaining one

down on an individual slip of paper and keep on choosing, this time blindly, until all chores are distributed. This system will, of course, need some adjustment where there are small children. Now you have a negotiated agreement in place that should carry all the weight of any rule on your list. Handle it as such, and expect compliance. You will probably get it; people (including kids) will be more inclined to support a program they have helped to design. One month later, go through the process again, unless there is a consensus that everyone is happy. They probably won't be, but it will be easier to deal with the second time around.

Now that you have dealt with the issues of allowance, compensation and chores, what else is there to negotiate? For most families, the main one is the matter of curfew. Most families have different standards for school nights and weekend evenings, and it seems as though there is often tension between children and parents on the limits that are set.

Negotiation begins with listening to each other and attempting to understand where each person is coming from. This may result in some accommodation to one another, and thus lay the groundwork for flexibility on deadlines where appropriate. From a parent's point of view, it might involve input from local police, and consultation with other parents, in an attempt to come up with some community standard acceptable beyond the family. Such a consensus is always easier to defend than an arbitrary one. While parents should be reluctant to dictate terms, they always have a right to refuse to accept proposed terms that are unacceptable.

Once agreements are made, they are enforceable until renegotiated; but how does a sleepy parent deal with—for instance—retiring before the kids get in? The most workable solution to this problem I have come across is for the parent to set an alarm clock to go off at the magic hour, and place it on the floor just outside the bedroom door. If it rings, and wakes Mom and Dad up, the son or daughter didn't make it home in time to shut it off—thus, they *were* out past their curfew!

Other items will need to be negotiated from time to time, but that should be relatively easy to do once an atmosphere of trust and respect has been established as a result of other successes. Work at it. Be patient. Show good faith, and it should work out okay.

Working with the School

Since all of us bring into adulthood a large number of vivid childhood memories, it should not be surprising to find that among these are recollections of experiences and activities associated with school. It would be most surprising if these impressions (negative and positive) exerted no influence upon our current attitudes toward school, education, homework, teachers and administrators. Therefore, let's try to be in touch with what is going on inside us as we try to deal with any school-related problems of our children.

It is easy for some parents to identify with, and almost become an extension of the school for their kids, and this can be very counterproductive. A clear distinction needs to be kept between parents and school in the minds of children. Always try to emphasize working *with* the school as a partner in a collaborative educational experience. Also consider the importance of working *with* your children on school matters. To make such a distinction positions the parent to serve as a buffer between school and child, if necessary, interpreting each to the other.

An example of this can be seen in situations where a child comes home somewhat upset over a school incident, claiming to have been misunderstood or treated unfairly by an adult.

Such a setting presents a temptation (that some parents can't resist) to lecture and preach—exactly what the child does not need! What is needed most is listening and understanding, without judgment or unsolicited advice, while the parent leaves responsibility for resolution of the problem in the hands of the child. In many cases, the young person needs only to sound off. On rare occasions it may be necessary for a parent to intervene on a child's behalf, but a decision to do so should almost always be a joint one.

There have been occasions recently when it might have been appropriate for me to get involved with the school on my son's behalf; but in every case, save one, after discussion, he decided on a way he could handle it by himself. And he did well.

But, if you are ever called in to the school for a conference, or receive an ugly note, or face a situation that calls for your prompt intervention, it is best if you do not respond as a stranger. It is also best if you do not respond alone, unless you are very confident, and you are already on good terms with the other person. It is not unusual for a parent to show up for a one-on-one conference, only to find him or herself across the table from two or more other persons. If, for whatever reason, two heads are better than one for the school, two heads are better than one for you. If both parents can't attend together, take a friend or relative; the reasons should be obvious.

So, here too, preventive maintenance is very useful. How do you do it? Get involved from the beginning of the school year; attend orientation programs and open-house opportunities. Take the initiative in getting to know the teachers, and offer to be available—as time permits—to do volunteer work. It will usually be deeply appreciated. When a teacher or other school employee does something above and beyond the call of duty, or just does something extremely well, be quick to recognize it. Be active in parent/teacher organizations. Share any special talents or interests that you have; many teachers are anxious to bring parents into their classrooms to talk about hobbies, professions or talents. When you are able to relate to the school in this way, you will find that it will be a real bonus for your child or children, too; they will be proud to have you involved and known.

Then, if a problem does develop involving your child, you will be likely to be contacted sooner, and the problem will be dealt with earlier. If you are unknown, a teacher may be reluctant to contact you until she feels it is really necessary, and this can mean the loss of valuable time in rectifying a situation that needs attention.

I recently received a newsletter from a school principal that pleased me greatly. In his column he encouraged parents to stay away from trying to push kids who were having trouble with a subject or who were short on motivation, lest such efforts be counterproductive. He suggested that he and his teachers were experts trained in dealing with these matters, and that they should be contacted if a parent spotted a problem before the school did. This viewpoint stood in refreshing contrast to the more traditional school posture of advising parents of a problem in such a way as to convey the message that *they* had discovered this problem, but it is *your* problem; now what do *you* intend to do about it.

I encourage parents to accept this principal's philosophy, rather than to accept complete responsibility for what is clearly the school's primary responsibility. It is always a refreshingly liberating idea for them. And when parents respond to school notifications by requesting an appointment and asking the school how they propose to deal with the problem, parents are often met by stunned silence, but it is always followed by complete cooperation. It gives some parents a new lease on life to learn that they are not totally responsible for the success of their children in school—or anywhere else for that matter!

This also explains what was said earlier on the subject of homework: *Children are responsible for ... completing their own school work (although we shall be glad to help if asked) ... They will not be bugged by us.* (House Rules, Rule #10)

If there is bugging to be done, let the school do it; you definitely have more to lose if you do it at home. Work *with* both the school and your kids, and things should go a lot smoother for everyone.

Over the past several years most guidance counselors, school psychologists and social workers have become extremely well trained and qualified for their work. They are valuable resource persons, and are anxious to be of assistance to students and their parents. In many schools they lead support groups for students with special needs, such as for children whose parents are going through a divorce. So, by all means, get to know these staff persons, too. You never know when you may need their services.

Time and Space

Most of what was said in Part One about the importance of young people having a strong power base and keeping their batteries charged is equally applicable to parents. While this is not a book on having a good marriage, the issues are not completely different. Everything seems to be so connected to everything else that it is difficult to know exactly where to draw the lines that separate one subject from another. Read through this section again, and consider how you are doing in terms of your own identity.

Specifically, parents and children not only need separate time and space on a daily basis, but for extended periods as well. I am amazed at the number of parents who stopped getting away together after they started a family. They either seem to feel they owe their children every free minute, or they don't trust another person to care for their kids. Change that now, or you may find that by the time the kids are *old enough* for you to do it, you are no longer interested.

A healthy marriage is a delicate, dynamic interaction between two changing persons. *Make* time to nurture yours. If you are single, make time to care for yourself in whatever way it takes to keep your own batteries charged. This may be a short, simple message, but it is a very important one; don't overlook it.

Consulting a Professional

As I've said before, I dislike the terms *counselor, therapist* and *psychotherapist; professional* seems more appropriate here. Whatever term you use, the time may come when you feel the need for the services of someone more experienced and knowledgeable than you. Most of us have little difficulty consulting physicians, accountants or attorneys; but for help with a personal, marital or family problem it's different—especially for men.

In the area of marriage and family concerns, a professional presumably has advanced education, membership in one or more appropriate societies, and a license or certificate from the state to offer his or her services for a fee.

Shaw once cautioned that, "Any professional society represents a conspiracy against laymen." A more delicate way to say this might be that no level or amount of credentials can offer anything more than presumptive evidence of competence. This means only that there are a number of additional things you will want to check out about a prospective professional before an initial meeting, as well as some things you will want to find out when you meet face to face for the first time—all *before* you commit to anything more than a preliminary consultation. For starters, then, let's ask ourselves when to consult a professional.

When Should You Call a Professional?—One should not wait until he is terminally ill to prepare a will. Neither should one wait until there is an emergency in the family before looking for someone to render professional assistance. Prudence and an interest in preventive maintenance suggest otherwise.

Once you succeed in establishing a working relationship with a professional person, it is a lot easier in time of need to pick up the phone and schedule a new appointment with an old friend than to start from scratch with a total stranger.

An additional factor which supports such an approach is the emphasis these days on short-term, goal-oriented intervention on the part of mental health care professionals, with the insurance companies insisting on highly focused treatment, in an effort to contain skyrocketing costs. This might be compared to the difference between the cost of a major overhaul for a badly neglected family auto, versus occasional tune-ups as needed.

For What Reason?—Preceding the specific rules proposed in *Rights, Duties, Privileges, Gratuities*, we included a statement that says you will consult a professional in the event that negotiating or renegotiating one or more rules reaches a stalemate. This is one of the best reasons for consulting a professional—simply because someone in the family wants to. It might only be for mediation, but even so, conflict resolution is never easy if you haven't been trained to do it. Until your family is able to do it on its own, a successful experience in conflict resolution with a professional can be a valuable learning experience for the whole family. Of course, a request to see a professional might involve something more complicated.

From the point of view of a parent, professional assistance might be sought if the system proposed in this books breaks down, or fails to work as it should. This should not necessarily happen, but it does from time to time, and one should not give up and throw out the whole package without trying to find out what went wrong.

Another good reason for consulting a professional is an unresolved conflict between a parent or parents and a child or children. Failure to nip this in the bud might make for greater problems later on for the entire family.

Then there are major life issues with which a couple or a whole family might need assistance: death or illness of a family member or close friend; relocation of a parent because of job requirements, especially if it's accompanied by a lengthy separation; loss of a job, especially when combined with a need for radical changes in family lifestyle; relocation of the entire family for employment reasons, resulting in changes in schools and loss of friends; parental conflict that is moving toward separation or divorce. There are others. The point is that you should seek assistance whenever you see a rocky road ahead and you don't know exactly how you can negotiate it successfully. Ask for help while there is still time, so that you and your family do not end up like Humpty Dumpty—broken and unable to be put back together again.

Concerns over a specific child might also trigger a parental request for professional assistance. Such issues as delinquent or unusual behavior; substance abuse; sudden changes in mood, eating patterns, sleep habits, school grades or personality; chronic problems with other children; tics; excessive concern about one's gender, or one's identity. If your child suffers from mental retardation or a developmental disorder, it will hopefully have already been identified and dealt with prior to adolescence. In some cases, however, these conditions escape detection earlier in life, and professional advice is warranted. In short, anything out of the ordinary that is not transient, and especially something that cannot be talked about and resolved within the family, is a good reason to find a professional to help.

Who Is Available?—There are many kinds of professionals working with couples and families. With some it is a sideline in a larger practice; with others it is a specialty. Some devote full-time to it; for others it is a part-time interest. Some work in a private practice; others are affiliated with a clinic or group. Some have a high overhead and charge correspondingly high fees; others work out of their homes and charge significantly less. Some are married; others are single, divorced or gay. Some are nearing retirement; others are fresh out of school. Some are licensed by the state; others are still training and work only under the supervision of a fully credentialed person. Some have children of their own; others do not. Some are accessible between sessions; others have unlisted telephone numbers. Some will respond gladly to questions on the telephone before making an initial appointment; others communicate with potential clients only through secretaries. Some are qualified to receive reimbursements from your insurance carrier; others are not. Psychologists routinely refer clients to medical specialists when appropriate; physicians often limit their referrals to those within the medical community. Some only see patients/clients on weekdays; others have evening and weekend hours. These are examples of the kind of things you may want to check out.

Professionals who work with couples and families are also found in different disciplines: medicine (psychiatry, pediatrics, family practice, geriatrics), the ministry, social work, psychology, law, school guidance, and finally marriage and family therapy. In other words, while people in various other disciplines may engage in marriage and family therapy in addition to or as a part of their primary discipline, there is a separate discipline for practitioners who work exclusively in the field. In addition, some professionals hold dual credentials, being fully trained and licensed in two different but closely related fields, such as marriage and family therapy plus one of the other professions mentioned.

There are two professional accrediting associations, both with high standards, that you should keep in mind.

The American Association for Marriage and Family Therapy, in Washington, DC. You can get informative literature on the organization and its membership standards, as well as the names of some members in your area by calling their offices.

The American Psychiatric Association is also headquartered in Washington, DC. There are a number of subdivisions in this professional society, including the Division of Family Psychology, and the Division of Child, Youth and Family Services. Any psychologist can join these divisions simply on the basis of interest. For those who choose to specialize in the area, there is the possibility of earning a diploma from the American Board of Examiners in Professional Psychology. This organization is separate from the American Psychological Association, but information, standards and names from either of these groups is also only a phone call away.

How Do I Choose?—Perhaps the best way to choose a professional to help your family is with the satisfied-customer approach. Make discrete inquiries of your friends, or ask for a recommendation from some other professional person you know, such as a school psychologist, social worker or guidance counselor. In some cases, especially with Health Maintenance Organizations (HMOs), you should consult your insurance carrier for some suggestions.

Then check the Yellow Pages under *Marriage and Family Counselors*. Look for some of the things mentioned above: professional affiliation, dual credentials, licensure, office hours. If you need more names, call one of the organizations that accredit professionals—such as the two already mentioned.

By this time, you'll have a few names with which to begin your search. Arrange them in the order they are to be called. Make a list of the questions you want to ask when you reach these people or their representatives. Then start dialing.

When you make an appointment, adopt a wait-and-see attitude. After an hour together you should have some idea of whether or not you want to try to work together. If you're not sure, shop around. Then go for it, and good luck!

You should not necessarily bypass your family physician in any of this. In fact some insurance carriers, especially HMOs, require you to consult with with your *primary care physician*. He or she is a key person in your family health care. Therefore, whenever there is a problem with a child that you feel might have some medical component, be sure to check with your physician first, but unless he or she is a most unusual person (or your insurance requires referrals to come through your family doctor), don't expect a referral to anyone other than another physician.

Physicians, especially specialists, depend upon their network of colleagues for referrals, without which they would soon be out of business. Clinical psychologists, on the other hand, are well trained in diagnostic procedures, and routinely refer to other medical personnel when appropriate.

Postscript and Caveat—Professionals within the health care industry are not necessarily the only sources of support and help with marital and family problems. Self-help groups have proliferated, and can represent a valid resource. Don't ignore this possibility if you have the time and energy to attend meetings and investigate these options within your community. Your local library and newspapers are a good source of information on what is available.

If there are no such groups nearby, consider joining forces with other concerned parents, school personnel or civic leaders to get one started (to deal with parenting issues, for example). If you can have about fifteen people present for a meeting, you should have little difficulty getting an appropriate professional person to make a presentation and lead a discussion on a subject of your choosing. No fee should be offered or expected. Some professionals have even been known to act as advisors to such groups—again, as a community service.

More on Divorce

This information is in addition to what was included in *When Parents Part Ways*, and it is especially important for parents who are still married to each other.

We have grown to think of divorce as an event that casts a long shadow over the future of everyone who is affected by it. Therefore, we tend to focus on the negative impact of that event upon children.

Recent long-term research with British children of divorced parents encourages us to see divorce more as a process than an event. This process begins with an earlier breakdown in the relationship of the parents, well before the actual divorce. During this stage it might be said that the parents became emotionally divorced (a term that has been in use in this country for some time). It is in this pre-divorce stage that children's subsequent divorce-related problems are really rooted. Looking back to that period, one can even see early signs of them.

A few of you will argue with this hypothesis, but it certainly raises a real concern over the mental health of families. It means that if roughly half the marriages in this country are failing, then approximately half of the nation's children are at risk, living as they are in families that are being held together by couples whose parenting abilities are seriously impaired. No wonder so many divorced parents report that their really big regret is that they waited so long to end their marriages.

While I am opposed to the idea that parents should *stay together for the sake of the children,* I am almost fanatic about the importance of family-life education for young people planning marriage, parenting education for couples expecting their first child, communication and human relations training for all adults and young people and further subsequent education at appropriate times during the life cycle. There is already a lot being done in these areas by different concerned institutions and organizations, including the schools, but it is not enough. And, we know that the ones who are not being touched by existing programs are generally the ones who need it most.

This clearly suggests certain things for parents:

1. Take family-life education seriously.
2. Work hard at developing and maintaining happy homes.
3. Lose no time in seeking professional assistance with problems you are unable to resolve quickly between yourselves.
4. Start early, letting your children know that you believe in premarital counseling, including psychological testing, and that you will help with the cost, if necessary.
5. Join forces with others who share your values, in an attempt to raise the consciousness of the entire community on these vital issues.

Additional Brief Issues

More on Love

Why isn't love enough; why do we need all these rules; why can't we just live by the Golden Rule? There are at least two possible answers to these questions. Let's look at them.

First, maybe love would be adequate if the nature of love were more fully understood and consistently practiced by all. But that utopian dream world isn't even remotely on the horizon yet. While we wait for it, some guidelines are needed to protect us from ourselves and to protect the lovers from the users. Lovers tend to give too much, and users tend to take all they can get. A structure can offer some protection for both, which will hopefully give the user a better chance to grow up.

~ ~ ~

> After nine years of drug addiction and alcohol abuse, which included treatment attempts by five different psychiatrists and three hospitals, a woman attacked her husband with a butcher knife while he was asleep in bed. (There had been two previous knife attacks, but they were made in broad daylight.) He disarmed her and locked her in the basement family room until morning, when he released her and announced his intention of going immediately to his attorney to initiate divorce proceedings. Her cynical response still rings in his ears, "Ha ha ha—I know you better than that; you don't have the nerve!"
>
> He thought he had shown love by his patience, while she held him in contempt for what she perceived to be his

weakness in letting her get away with it. After almost two subsequent years of virtual isolation (She had alienated her friends and four children.) she quit her drugs and alcohol—completely on her own and without *any* professional help—and gradually became her old self again. Had her husband set some limits and shown less tolerance when it all started, their 23-year marriage might not have ended in divorce.

~ ~ ~

A second response to the question is to suggest that for some parents, it just seems easier to do nothing than to try to make changes, even though the proposed changes offer a hope for better times. So, a professed love can easily be a cover for laziness, or indifference, or selfishness, or even some fatalistic religious notion that *all things work together for good* regardless of what one does or fails to do.

Power Sharing

Have you ever seen two partners who were equally submissive? It is a strange sight to behold, because they can become so paralyzed that decisions are all but impossible, with each being angry at the other for being so indecisive.

The other extreme is equally frustrating to deal with: two powerful persons, neither of whom is willing to share power with the other. Each feels threatened by the other, and each tends to see the other as a competitor. Although difficult for a professional to *fix*, it is much easier than correcting the former condition. Obviously, they must learn to share power. Once they are able to do this, a really fine relationship is possible, for neither one has to feel completely responsible for the whole thing any longer. They can then relax and begin to enjoy complementing each other in a true partnership.

I won't even try to explain how to do this; Tom Gordon has already done a superb job of it in his book, *Parent Effectiveness Training,* which I reviewed in the *Constructive Communication* chapter.

The main reason for addressing the issue of power sharing here is this: if dominance is a trait of either parent (or both), it will probably show up in the children, and could easily be labeled as stubbornness or defiance—something to be challenged and suppressed. Be on guard against this pitfall, for we know from experience that the characteristics we dislike most in our children are often those we like least in ourselves or the other parent.

Affirm and encourage strength in your children, and show them by example and teaching how to develop and channel that strength constructively. Learn how to resolve conflicts so that everyone wins and no one loses; to refuse to share power with your partner and children forces *everyone* to become a loser.

But, you may say, isn't power what this whole system is all about? In a way, it certainly is; but there is a distinction to be made here that is very important. I'll illustrate it with a story.

~ ~ ~

> I once had a colleague who wanted me to do something for her that I couldn't possibly agree to, for ethical reasons; and I courteously declined. It was not an outrageous request, just something unacceptable to me on personal grounds. That took place 15 years ago, but I still remember how shocked I was at her reaction, because I really thought she knew better (as a professional who presumably understood these things). She became very angry and accused me of trying to control her with my power, just because I could not grant her request. She never did understand, and I think that incident probably marked the beginning of the end for our relationship.

~ ~ ~

We have certain obligations toward our children which were discussed in Part One; but beyond that it's *yes* or *no*, as we see fit, depending upon any number of factors. I think that posture represents a legitimate use of power. And when others start to badger us over our gratuitous decisions, that represents an attempted power play on *their* part. The same goes for friends, spouses, other relatives and employers.

Being a Good Consultant

Some parents think that as our children grow older, they need us less. I prefer to think that they continue to need us, but in different ways. If we fail to adjust to those shifting ways, we may indeed find that they need us less. Understanding the role of the consultant may give us a model for relating to our children throughout the whole process of growing up.

A consultant is defined as *an expert who is called on for professional or technical advice or opinions.* That's you! And even if your kids don't call on you very often for advice or opinions, you can still be a consultant to them. How? Simply by asking. With my own children, their curiosity always got the best of them, causing them to wonder what it was I wanted to say. Consequently, I was never refused.

An approach might go something like one of these:

1. "May I offer an opinion on that subject?"
2. "I have a piece of advice I'd like to pass on, if you're willing to listen."
3. "With your permission, I'd like to respond to what you said."
4. "I've given a lot of thought to what you said about (whatever) and would really appreciate a chance to react to it."
5. "I'd like to sound off about something. Care to listen?"

As Tom Gordon points out in his books, a consultant makes the clearest and most persuasive presentation he or she can make, together with whatever recommendations seem appropriate, then the consultation is finished. The consultant may never know what action was taken, but his or her job has been completed.

For best results with our children, we need to present any recommendations as options, and preferably no less than two. This leaves the young person free to choose, and reduces fear of disappointing a parent.

The consultant role is important in dealing with values, and especially with behaviors taking place outside the home—over which parents of teenagers have very little real control.

A really nice thing about this model is that you can use it even after the kids are grown and you are biting your tongue instead of offering recommendations on child rearing. It works! I've used it, and seen it in use by my wife on an almost daily basis, with absolutely great results.

A good example of a special situation in which this approach is indispensable is when a youngster says ...

I Want to Quit School

It should be fairly easy to see something like this coming, but when the words finally are spoken, it is inevitably sobering and upsetting. Parents see all kinds of probable consequences that the young person hasn't seen, or else doesn't care to see.

What do you do about it? Let's consider first how to prevent it.

Occasionally, a learning disability or developmental disorder of some kind slips by unnoticed in the early years. The longer these problems go without being identified, the harder it is to deal with them, and the harder it is on the child's self-esteem. So keep a watchful eye on your child's school progress, and insist on adequate evaluations (in the private sector if necessary) before you accept the comment, "He'll probably grow out of it; I'm sure it's just a stage he's going through."

There are different ways to get an education, and there are no excuses these days for failing to design programs to meet the needs of children who, for some reason, are not completely suited to traditional mainstream learning.

Again, a story—this one about a heroic and devoted aunt.

~ ~ ~

> The woman's nephew had been placed in a state *school* for the severely disabled. (A people warehouse might have been a better name for it.) She refused to believe his situation was hopeless, and she obtained permission to care for him in her home. She worked with him on a daily basis with passive exercises and massage for his physical handicap. He appeared to be autistic, and could only make noises at first. Gradually she established contact, and was able to provide him with a reason to try, and together they worked, year after year.
>
> He was an adult when I first met him, and absolutely the only noticeable handicap he had was a slight speech impediment. He worked for the postal service, continued to live with his aunt, and was an active church worker. A more caring and thoughtful person I have never met than Elmer.

~ ~ ~

I wonder sometimes how many other lives might have been salvaged, had the right person only come along in time to make a difference. So stay on top of anything out of the ordinary, and do what you can as a persistent advocate for your child, to get the services that are needed.

But if in spite of all that you do (including getting professional assistance), your child is still determined to quit school, for whatever reason, what can you do? You obviously can't make a kid learn; in fact, you can't even make him attend school in most states after age 16.

~ ~ ~

A mother, father, and their 16-year-old daughter were referred to me because she refused to attend school any longer. The parents were sure that it was a bad decision, and were equally confident that I would be able to pull some trick out of my bag that would convince her of the folly of her ways, and get her to return to the classroom.

She listened respectfully to all the reasons given by her parents, politely rejecting every one. She said she valued an education and would definitely finish high school on her own, a prospect her parents considered very unlikely. She wanted to get a full-time job—something else the parents thought to be unlikely for a girl her age.

At this point the parents were not acting like good consultants, for they were continuing to hassle their daughter. This was understandable, but counterproductive. I suggested that they accept their daughter's decision (which is partly what consulting is all about) and consider instead what it was that she expected from them. This changed the focus of the discussion, and they were able to engage in some trade-offs.

They decided to accept her decision to leave school, and agreed that she could continue to live at home *if* she first: found a full-time job; enrolled in a local G.E.D. program geared to help school dropouts earn their diplomas; agreed to continue to live by their house rules; and, agreed to pay a certain amount from her wages for room and board.

Although she agreed to their terms, they did not expect her to be able to fulfill her end of the bargain. In this case, she surprised them (and me) by getting a job as a waitress in a nice local restaurant. She also signed up for a G.E.D. program, completing it so quickly that she had to wait to get her diploma until her class caught up with her. In fact, she graduated with them—cap and gown, and all. Rather unusual I would say, but that's an example of parents being good consultants, and a daughter knowing what she wanted. In this story they all came out winners.

~ ~ ~

Not everyone who says he or she wants to quit school really wants to quit. The statement is often indicative of a problem which needs attention, and which can be resolved with the help and cooperation of the school, and other professionals if necessary.

Hopefully, you will never have to deal with something like this, but if you should, there may be some helpful ideas here.

Odds and Ends

One on One—I had just left my two daughters in Fairborn, Ohio for a visit with friends, and was driving with my 5- and 9-year-old boys back to our home in Dover, Delaware. We had not traveled far before I began to wonder who in the world the kid was in the back seat, for he was chattering with his brother and me as I had never heard him carry on before. I began to see a side of him that I had never seen—and it was very strange.

It wasn't hard to figure out what was going on: he didn't have to compete with two older sisters for attention! The older sister was 14, and was known appropriately among her friends as Motormouth. (She had won a speed spelling contest in school with *supercalifragilisticexpialidocious*.) With his brother David was okay, but with his sisters, he didn't stand a chance.

I suddenly realized that whatever time I had spent with him to date included the other three kids as well. I must have spent *some* alone time with him, I tried to tell myself, but to no avail. I couldn't believe it.

I determined to correct that immediately, and did. And I am glad that I did!

~ ~ ~

If you miss out on one-on-one time with your kids, you'll miss a real opportunity to relate to them in unique ways.

Prenuptial Agreements—If you are a single parent and decide to remarry, and especially if you marry a partner who is also a parent, you will probably want to consider the possible need for a prenuptial agreement. Lawyers are divided on the issue, and perhaps this is not too surprising. I include comments on the subject here because of the possible impact such an agreement (or lack of one) might have upon your children, in the event of the dissolution of a second marriage.

To suggest such a possibility is not that outlandish, because the divorce rate for second marriages is almost the same as for first-time marriages. And, as I mentioned previously, the children seem to be a major source of the discord that contributes to the breakdown of the relationship.

There are many variables that bear upon a decision to propose a prenuptial agreement—probably too many for me to try to identify here. So I won't try. Instead, I would urge anyone considering remarriage to become familiar with the literature on the subject, including all the pros and cons. Also, I would strongly urge an individual consultation on the subject with one's attorney before making a final decision.

Dealing with a Former Spouse—If you have a former spouse, you could write this section yourself. If you're not in that category, consider yourself lucky; and read on if you think it might one day apply. Following are some general rules of thumb, to which there might conceivably be an occasional exception under very special circumstances:

1. Former spouses have no place in your present home—not even in inclement weather or to pick up kids. It confuses the kids; it's upsetting for you; and your new spouse (if you have one) will feel violated.
2. You should deal with your ex and let your new spouse deal with his or hers, except in emergencies. If you must have a conference with an ex, let

it be in a public place. It's safer that way. If an argument develops, immediately get up and leave.

3. The same goes for telephone consultations. Stick with business, and hang up without comment if an argument develops.
4. The judges I know would like to see separated or divorced parents be able to share joint custody of their children, because it is so much better for everyone. But if it were that easy, the parents would probably still be married. After both are remarried, and some time has passed (a year or two), it is often easier to get along with an ex. Until then it may at times be difficult. A wise person once said, "When there are children, divorce doesn't end a relationship; it only changes it."
5. Do everything possible to protect your children from becoming involved in parental conflicts. Listen courteously to anything they have to say, but never join with them in bashing the other parent.

Some Closing Words

How do we measure parental success or failure? Is it even right or appropriate to think in such terms? What criteria might we use in such an evaluation? And what about the person whose ability to be a better parent is impaired or limited by factors totally beyond his or her control? Do social, economic, cultural, educational, racial, geographic and ethnic factors have any impact upon success or failure? What about a child's genetic limitations, if any? And what about the child's exercise of his or her freedom to choose and make decisions? Also, is it okay to have dreams for our children? And if so, what kind?

When we think in terms of the above questions, it becomes easier to agree with whomever it was who said, "Parents don't fail; sometimes they just don't succeed."

But again, succeed in what? If we had fewer expectations, might we feel less of that nagging sense that we did something wrong, or failed to do more that was good or right?

On the other hand, if we reduce our expectations, how far can we go before we become indifferent—possibly like Andy Capp, who was accused by Flo of being a failure. He responded with, "How can I be, woman; I never tried!"

To be philosophical takes time: more time than most of us have. Free time has become a rare commodity that few parents enjoy, *especially* single parents. In fact, I know of *no* single parent whose life is completely satisfying—primarily because of the time factor.

So what can the conscientious parent do? Frankly, I don't know what more can be expected of any of us than that we always try to do the best we can with what we have at any particular time.

It may also help to remember that a lot of really great and fine people have come out of conditions and circumstances that were far from ideal. In other words, the most important contribution we make to the well-being of our children is not in the area of tangible things, but rather in the area of values: the attitudes, behaviors and feelings we exhibit that affect the quality of our children's lives. This thought was expressed very well in a recent issue of *The Harvard Mental Health Letter,* by Dr. E. James Lieberman, who said, "Honest, loving family ties are the ... greatest security in an uncertain world."

And with that thought I shall conclude this book, and leave you to your kids. Happy parenting!

Appendix A

FAMILY DISCUSSION GUIDELINES

This section is designed for parents, and includes material for home discussion groups that was referenced earlier. It can be adapted to other settings, but it is presented here for family use.

In the introductory material to this book, and again in the chapter *If Not You, Who? If Not Now, When?*, we discussed the possibility of resistance to the system presented here from other family members. But whether or not your children drag their feet, there will be the need for a great deal of supportive listening and understanding on your part, together with the reassurance that their feelings are important to you. Emphasize the positive aspects of participation, which basically add up to this: they will get a much better deal if everyone makes an effort to pull together, thus making this a joint effort.

When it comes to getting children to share their true feelings on a given subject—as opposed to saying what they think someone else wants to hear—a little candor on your part will be helpful in terms of modeling the kind of behavior you expect from them. So, don't be afraid of being honest—and thus becoming vulnerable. Talk about what it was like when you were a child. What were your fears and worries? What kinds of conflicts did you have with your parents, and how were they handled? Talk, but not too much—certainly not more than your fair share of the time. Be respectful, and try not to contradict.

Sometimes discussions can range far afield. Don't worry too much about this, as long as it is what everyone wants to do.

One useful technique, which was mentioned earlier, is for you all to take turns reading this book aloud. Continue your reading until someone has a comment or question. Stop there and pursue that concern until there is a consensus to move on. If you want the children to value this experience, be sure to get them all involved in the process.

You may already be a skilled and experienced group facilitator, with no need for any suggestions. If so, allow yourself to be innovative, flexible and imaginative; and please don't be bound by what follows. Under other circumstances, it may be possible for two adults to co-lead a discussion group; but it is preferable for only one person at a time to moderate, rotating this responsibility with the change of topics, if desired.

In the following chapter-by-chapter compilation of comments and suggested questions, the headings correspond to the comparable sections in Part One.

Preface

Suggestions on structure:

1. Before starting to read this book together—
   a. Complete the following statement aloud, and invite everyone else to do likewise in turn: "One thing I really like about our family is ____________." Record the responses and hold on to them.
   b. Then do the same with this staement: "One thing I'd really like to see change in our family is ______________." Record these responses and hold on to them.
2. After reading and discussing this section, make note of any loose ends or unanswered questions. Hold on to these for future reference. Some questions may anticipate subsequent material. In that case, reassurance that the concern will eventually be addressed is important.
3. Try to conclude the discussion with something like:
   a. "Are there any other comments or questions on this section before we move on to the next unit?"
   b. "Is there anything we need to do, or is there any homework we need to accomplish before our next meeting?"
   c. "Where and when shall we meet next? And for how long?"

4. Record and retain anything of significance for possible future use.
5. Item numbers 2, 3 and 4 above will provide a workable ritual for concluding a discussion on any of the chapters in this book. Use it or adapt it to whatever works for you, as long as it makes for smooth transitions between sessions.

About Part One

More suggestions on structure:

1. Establish a comfortable opening routine which flows logically from the closing of the previous discussion. This might include:
   a. "Do we have anything left over from our previous meeting—agenda of any kind, projects, homework? If so, let's take a look at it."
   b. "Any further thoughts or comments on the previous material that anyone might like to share?"
   c. "Any personal updates or any other comments before we begin reading?"
2. Use these guidelines for beginning any group. And since I've already shared suggestions for closing a session, I'll refrain from further reference to opening and closing activities.

Comment: This chapter seems to be self-explanatory. Just discuss it as you go.

Some Basics

Here are some possible questions that may not be covered adequately during your reading and discussion:

1. "How does it feel to be told that you are wrong?"
2. "How do you want to react when that happens?"
3. "How does it feel when you're given a direct order?"

4. "Describe a better way to gain your cooperation?"
5. "Can you think of other ways to respond to unacceptable or unpleasant orders than by being defiant?"
6. "Under what circumstances is it acceptable to give an order?"

Suggestion: If it seems appropriate and feels okay, consider the possibility of telling your children that you want to make a real effort to cut down on orders. Ask them to remind you when you goof.

Where Did I Go Wrong?

Possible questions:

1. "Do you feel that you understand us (your parents) any better as a result of reading this chapter?"
2. "Would you like me to tell you what I've learned from reading this chapter (if appropriate)?"
3. "In the light of this chapter, I wonder if there are behaviors that we need to work on changing. For example, I think I could work on my tendency to (whatever)." Others will be impressed by this and will hopefully follow your example. Furthermore, you'll be ahead of the game by identifying your own agenda rather than waiting for the kids to point out to you where you have become rusty. Who can listen to that from children without getting defensive?
4. "When one of us slips up, how can the rest of us call it to his or her attention without being ugly or unpleasant?"

Suggestion: All four of these questions are probably appropriate for use with several of the chapters in Part One. Therefore, you might want to retain them for possible future use. In my future comments, I'll assume as much and not repeat them.

Gladly Will I Toil and Suffer

Observation: There's some heavy stuff in this chapter. After reading and discussing it together, just remember to use the questions suggested earlier to probe what was learned.

Homework:

1. Be sure *you* read the next chapter in advance. Also, skip forward and read the first subsection called *Expectations* in the *Selected Commentary on Part One* chapter.
2. Invite everyone to prepare for the next meeting by making a list of what they expect from friends and family. This may take a little explaining. Point out that they should be willing to subscribe to whatever standard it is that they establish for others. What we're looking for here is something that is fair, that the entire family can accept and live with.

If You Love Me You Will

Suggestions:

1. As a part of your preliminaries, inquire about the homework and get a feel for how much was accomplished. Then proceed with your reading and discussion until you reach the section *Expectations.*
2. At that point you may want to invite others to share and compare their lists, or see if you can collectively develop a list from scratch for your family, to which you can all subscribe. Or you may decide to proceed directly with a discussion of the book's list.
3. When you do get to it, it would be useful to go over the points carefully, making sure each one is understood. Solicit comments. The goal is to achieve a consensus; it may be necessary to engage in some minor revision. You may even choose to delete #9 completely for now. And you may add one or more of your own.

4. When the list is complete, have it typed and let everyone sign and receive a copy of it. These are not rules to be enforced; rather, they represent a collective civilized standard to which every family member subscribes. They are what each one pledges to give to, and expect from, the others.

Possible questions:

1. "Are we clear as to the distinction between self-love and selfishness?"
2. "Are we all clear on the difference between *doing* something stupid and *being* a stupid person?"
3. "Is there any more work we need to do on our list of expectations?"

I Can't Trust You Anymore

1. If you can subscribe to the mother's letter that appears just before the subsection on lying, say so—it will probably be deeply appreciated. If you can't, just say that you need more time to think about it. Maybe you can then revise it into a form that you *can* accept.
2. Thoroughly discuss the subsection on lying, especially with reference to that list of eight optional responses to questions. Can you all agree to accept them when used by other members of the family? If so, there should be no further need for lying by anyone.

Possible questions:

1. "With respect to a power base, how about describing our individual power bases as we see them? I'll go first. After each of us speaks, let others identify assets that the speaker might have overlooked."
2. "We're half way through the book. How are we doing so far?"

Homework:

1. The next chapter is also one that you are well advised to read in advance, as well as the second subsection of *Selected Commentary on Part One* on rules.
2. Now is the time to review carefully that model list of house rules in the next chapter, adapting it to the needs of your family. Remember—these are *your* responsibility, legally and morally. They are not to be designed jointly. Have the list ready for the next session. But remember, there are other negotiable rules to be dealt with later.
3. This next assignment, which is for your children, is taken right out of the book: divide a sheet of paper into two columns. In the left-hand column make a list of your rights; in the right-hand column, list all the privileges you have, either things you are permitted to do for yourself or things your parents do for you.

Rights, Duties, Privileges, Gratuities

Comment: This is a very important chapter—one that you may well work on for more than one session. Just break wherever it seems appropriate, and do a little review before picking it up at the following meeting. This chapter is designed to make your task a lot easier by giving your children a clear rationale for the structure you are establishing.

Suggestions:

1. Work on the children's homework assignment as part of your preliminaries. If it hasn't been completed, take time to do it in the group meeting. Then, encourage the children to share and discuss their lists, without making any pronouncements of your own. When all are ready, just suggest that the reading and discussion begin. You might say, "Let's see what our book has to say on the subject."

2. Some kids hold an inappropriate amount of power, which they do not want to lose. Here is where such a youngster may get scared and show some resistance. Don't panic or argue. Just listen. There does seem to be a mystique and power to the printed word, so plug ahead and hope for the best. Just take the necessary time to discuss and digest each section carefully as you go.
3. When you come to the list of eight reasons for having house rules, take your time. Ask, "Do you understand this? Does it make sense to you?"
4. When you come to the section *House Rules,* just go ahead with your discussion—paragraph by paragraph, and rule by rule.—without any reference to your own list. By the time you finish discussing rule #15, you'll know whether or not you are ready to present your list. You may want to do some polishing. You may have some ideas you had not considered prior to the discussion. If so, just tell the kids that you are still working on your list, and that it will be ready next time.
5. When discussing the section on privileges, you may need to take some extra time. The paragraph that begins, "You enjoy a number of privileges and benefits," should become the final paragraph in your own list of house rules. It is a very important statement. It is followed in the book by illustrative material calculated to convince kids that this plan is fair and makes sense.
6. I'm sure the car-use-request form story caught your attention. It works! Don't be afraid to use it.
7. Before you begin the section on gratuities, you may want to work on your negotiable rules (chores, curfew, allowance, meal time, quiet time). If so, refer to the applicable subsections in the *Selected Commentary on Part One* and *Additional Brief Issues* for guidance.

When Parents Part Ways

Comment: If your first marriage is intact, this chapter will have little relevance for your children, except to help them understand what some of their friends and relatives may have gone through; perhaps those interested in reading through it can do so on their own. On the other hand—if you are a single parent or a stepparent, it should prove to be very useful.

Suggestions:

1. As you read and discuss your way through this chapter, try to be sensitive to comments made by children, encourage them to elaborate where appropriate. Don't be reluctant to acknowledge something that may describe what you felt or are feeling. You might even ask the children if they have ever felt or experienced anything similar. Inquire gently, and back off immediately if there is resistance to discussion.
2. If yours is a stepfamily, you might choose to stop before reading the subsection *Which Family* to invite all present, including adults, to list the names of everyone in his or her family. Then discuss it, being supportive of everyone's list.
3. As you read about the different issues or concerns dealt with in this chapter, don't be afraid to ask, cautiously, if your family has ever dealt with these things. If so, ask, "Do we need to do any more work on it, or it it okay now?"

Constructive Communication

Observation: Although this chapter is brief, it is well worth reading together; it provides new information and suggests additional opportunities. For instance, by this time, you have developed some idea of the possibilities for group discussion that exist in your family. If you feel good about what you've done so far, you might want to consider promoting a Parent Effectiveness Training and/or a Youth Effectiveness Training course in your community at some future point. Or you may decide simply to finish reading and reviewing the book together first. Other group and individual study options will be identified in another part of the appendix.

Loose Ends

Suggestions:

1. This brings us to the last chapter in Part One. Use the earlier suggestions for preliminaries and closing, and go through this unit, subsection by subsection, digressing as may be necessary to accommodate the needs and interests of everyone. There should be good opportunities here for sharing and learning from one another. And what happens between you now may influence the possibilities for further group experiences of this type.
2. When you come to the section, *The Empty Nest,* don't hesitate to ask an older child if he or she has given any thought to the subject.
3. When you have completed your discussion of this chapter, you might want to expand your closing ritual to include a look at the entire experience, giving everyone an opportunity to react freely.
4. Next, deal with the question of where you go from here.

   a. How about meeting occasionally to discuss how you are doing as a family with the structure that is now in place. You'll probably want to do this at least monthly, to keep it from unraveling, and to deal with chores. It might be helpful if you could also agree to meet any time one family member has an concern that can't wait until the next scheduled meeting.

   b. Be sure that each family member has a personal copy of all the documents that have been generated in these meetings—especially those dealing with expectations, rules and chores.

c. Do you want to consider taking a break and then starting over again for a series of discussions focused on another book or program, such as one of those identified in the bibliography?

5. Be sure to thank everyone for his or her participation and cooperation. Deal with any other closing formalities you have developed, and conclude the meeting.

Reminder: Things don't just get done; somebody has to do them. So, expect members of your family to do what they say they're going to do. If they forget, and a gentle reminder doesn't correct it, you now know what you have to do.

Appendix B

HELP LINES

In the chapter *Selected Commentary on Part One*, subsection *Consulting a Professional*, we discussed how one might go about locating a person or agency to help with family problems. The following information will elaborate on and complement that earlier material. Telephone numbers and addresses do change, but prior to publication all of those listed here were checked and confirmed.

Agencies with toll-free numbers are listed here only if they are accessible throughout, and provide service to, the entire United States. Check a toll-free directory in your local library for other agencies and help lines which serve your state or limited geographic area.

Other local help lines can be found in the white pages of your local directory, following such lead words as *Alcohol, Drug Abuse, Crisis* and *Emergency.* Your local United Way office may also be a rich source of information, since many of them publish a directory of the nonprofit community agencies they help to support.

~ ~ ~

American Association for Marriage and Family Therapy
1100 Seventeenth Street, N.W., Tenth Floor
Washington, DC 20036 **1-202-452-0109**

AAMFT can also provide you with a telephone number for your state chapter, or a print-out of the therapists in your zip code area.

American Board of Examiners in Professional Psychology
2100 E. Broadway, Suite 313
Columbia, MO 65201 **1-314-875-1267**

This organization certifies psychologists in a number of specialties. They will provide you with the names of persons in your area who are diplomates in Family Psychology.

American Psychological Association
1200 Seventeenth Street, N.W.
Washington, DC 20036 **1-202-955-7600**

This office can give you the telephone number for your state psychological association, which in turn can offer you names of members in your area.

American Self-Help Clearing House
Denville, NJ 07834 **1-201-625-7101**

They provide telephone numbers for those states that have clearing houses for self-help groups. They also provide numbers for national headquarters and state chapters of specific nationwide self-help organizations. (Some states do not yet have information clearing houses, but those that do cover most large metropolitan areas.) There are an unbelievable number of groups in existence which focus on very specific needs (including rare disorders and illnesses), and this is where you can call to locate them. Following are just a few examples of better known sources that are listed.

1. Alcoholics Anonymous (AA): for alcoholics
2. AL-ANON: for family and friends of alcoholics
3. ALATEEN: for teens with an alcoholic family member
4. Families Anonymous: for situations where there is drug abuse or other related behavioral problems in the life of a family member
5. Mothers Against Drunk Driving (MADD): dedicated to keeping drunk drivers off the roadways
6. National Alliance for the Mentally Ill (NAMI): provides support, education and advocacy for families with an impaired member
7. Parents Without Partners (PWP): provides mutual support, education, recreation and social activities for single parents and their children
8. Sick Kids Need People (SKIP): assists families to procure needs and services to keep children with special health needs at home

9. Stepfamily Association of America: provides information and advocacy for stepfamilies
10. Tough Love: provides help for parents, kids and community when a family member is exhibiting out-of-control behavior

Boys Town National Hotline (24 hours)
Boys Town, NE 68010 **1-800-448-3000**

Crisis line for troubled parents and children. Short term telephone counseling offered; Spanish speaking counselors available. Offers referral to local programs and agencies nationwide. TDD line for hearing impaired : **1-800-448-1833.**

Covenant House
New York, NY **1-800-999-9999**

Nationwide crisis hot line serving parents and children in the United States and Canada, providing information and referrals to local agencies.

Effectiveness Training Associates
531 Stevens Avenue
Solana Beach, CA 92075-2093 **1-619-481-8121**

Information and literature available on the courses described in the chapter *Constructive Communication.*

National Health Information Center
Silver Spring, MD **1-800-336-4797**

Staffed by the Office of Disease Prevention and Health Promotion, under the United States Public Health Service. Provides automated access to prerecorded information on a variety of medical subjects. Also provides current telephone numbers for over 1,000 organizations (Federal agencies, professional societies, state health departments, specific disease-related interest groups and state clearing houses for information on self-help groups).

Appendix C

SUPPLEMENTARY RESOURCES

BOOKS

Adams, Caren, and Jennifer Fay and Jan Loreen-Martin. ***No Is Not Enough.*** San Luis Obispo: Impact, 1984.
Contains workable guidelines to help young people avoid sexual victimization.

Allen, Juliet V. ***What to Do When.*** San Luis Obispo: Impact, 1983.
A practical handbook for dealing with a host of specific problem behaviors in children of all ages.

Bartz, Wayne R., and Richard A. Rasor. ***Surviving with Kids*** San Luis Obispo: Impact, 1978.
Behavior oriented discussion of thirty principles for understanding and handling children of all ages.

Becker, Wesley C. ***Parents Are Teachers.*** Champaign, IL: Research Press, 1971.
This volume has been used successfully as a text and workbook in Project Follow Through (a sequel to Head Start). Easy to read and understand. Primarily for use with younger children, but the principles are applicable to all ages.

Dinkmeyer, Don, and Gary D. McKay. ***Parenting Teenagers.*** Circle Pines, NM: American Guidance Service, 1983.
This is the parents' guide for STEP/teen (Systematic Training for Effective Parenting of Teens), a widely used parent education program. It is easy to read and very helpful. Explains where to get information on forming a STEP/teen study group.

Gardiner, Richard A. ***The Boys and Girls Book about Divorce.*** New York: Jason Aronson, 1970.

By a child psychologist, based on 13 years of clinical experience. Written to children, and well illustrated with drawings. Good introduction for parents. Designed to stimulate discussion between kids and adults.

Garvin, James P. ***Learning How to Kiss a Frog.*** New England League of Middle Schools, 460 Boston Street, Suite #4, Topsfield, MA 01983, 1988.

This is a comprehensive 38-page discussion of the essential characteristics of pre-and early-adolescents, by a seasoned educator. Easy to read and understand. Includes an extensive listing of books on human sexuality.

Gordon, Thomas. ***Parent Effectiveness Training.*** New York: Peter H. Wyden, 1970.

Reviewed in Constructive Communication chapter of this book.

—. ***P.E.T. in Action.*** New York: Peter H. Wyden, 1976.

An in-depth exploration—utilizing illustrative case studies—of what really happens when parents apply Parent Effectiveness Training in the home. Practical suggestions for a wide range of issues.

—. ***Discipline That Works.*** New York: Plume Books, 1989.

Discusses the futility of punitive disciplinary measures and shows how they produce anti-social behavior. Explores further his methods for raising self-reliant children.

Gross, Leonard, ed. ***The Parents' Guide to Teenagers.*** New York: Collier MacMillan, 1981.

Contains 385 pages of responses by over 300 authorities, to 323 questions parents have asked about teenagers. Good reference book.

Palmer, Pat, and Melissa Alberti Froehner. ***Teen Esteem.*** San Luis Obispo: Impact, 1989.

Designed to show young people how to build the attitudes and skills necessary for survival in today's world.

Schaefer, Charles E., and Howard L. Millman. ***How to Help Children with Common Problems.*** New York: Van Nostrand Reinhold Co., 1981.

A detailed and comprehensive treatment of a full range of behavioral problems from childhood to adolescence. Considers possible reasons for each behavior, and suggests different ways to deal with it. Also considers preventive child rearing strategies. For parents and professionals.

Schaefer, Charles E., and James M. Briesmeister, eds. ***Handbook of Parent Training.*** New York: Wiley, 1989.

Designed to serve as a practical and comprehensive guide for practitioners who deal with dysfunctional behaviors of children, this 500 page book has much to offer parents who are faced with situations which call for professional intervention. Could be very useful in helping parents to know what to look for in terms of treatment.

Simon, Sidney B., and Sally Wendkos Olds. ***Helping Your Child Learn Right from Wrong.*** New York: Simon and Schuster, 1976.

Dr. Simon adapts his values clarification program to families, showing how parents can teach children a process for arriving at their own values, in a collaborative and enjoyable way. No moralizing.

CATALOGS OF AUDIOVISUALS AND PUBLICATIONS

Boys Town Marketing Division
Boys Town, NE 68010 **1-402-498-3200**

Most of the materials are directed toward parents, many pamphlets offered free of charge. Videos are reasonably priced. Boys Town is expanding this service.

~ ~ ~

Impact Publishers
P.O. Box 1094
San Luis Obispo, CA 93406 **1-805-543-5911**

Self-help books in personal growth, relationships, families, communities and health.

~ ~ ~

Research Press, Dept. B
2612 North Mattis Avenue
Champaign, IL 61821 **1-217-352-3273**

While most of the materials in their catalog are designed for professionals, they offer a large variety of relevant video programs that your community or institutional library might be interested in purchasing.

Index